Hummels And Me

Hummels And Me

LIFE STORIES

Gerhard Skrobek

Portfolio Press
Huntington, New York

Published by Portfolio Press,
Huntington, New York

ISBN: 0-942620-18-6

Photo on front cover by
Michael Tonn, Neustadt bei Coburg

Printed and bound in the U.S.A.

This book is dedicated to my "Better Half," Sieglinde— without her, I would not be what I am.

Contents

In learning a foreign language, there are two different skills: speaking and reading a little in that language, and writing. I increased my knowledge of the English language during my travels in the United States, but not enough to write a book. So, I asked my old friend Wolf Brandt to translate my words, and he accepted. I must thank him very much for his excellent job.

Wolf Brandt emigrated from Germany in 1952. In 1968, he founded the well-known gift shop "Seven Dwarfs" in Kansas City, Missouri. He has sold M.I. Hummel figurines, and was a member of the advisory board of the W. Goebel Porzellanfabrik in Roedental, Germany.

The contents of this book are the personal opinions and recollections of Gerhard Skrobek and do not represent W. Goebel Porzellanfabrik.

Prologue

In the course of my frequent travels throughout the United States as master sculptor for the Goebel company, I have met many collectors who inquired, with genuine interest, about my life. While I have written articles for German newspapers and magazines, I am not a writer, and so I tell my story from the point of view of an artist.

During my life I have experienced the heights of happiness, the passions of inspiration, and the depths of despair. I was born in Germany in 1922, heir to a multi-million-dollar textile business, and spent the early years of my childhood living a carefree existence in upper-class luxury. To our servants, I was "the young master." Then, with the worldwide depression of 1929, came our fall into poverty—a devastating experience for a child. When conditions finally began to improve in the 1930s, the rise of the Nazis led to life-threatening persecution for our entire family.

In 1945, after we had lost everything in World War II, came a new start. The ensuing years proved difficult; our family was scattered all over the world, I struggled professionally and my marriage failed. All this tested my endurance, but I did not give up. Eventually a new and very happy marriage laid the foundation for my first professional successes, which were accompanied by critical recognition and public praise.

The rollercoaster of my life has only strengthened my purpose and understanding. I have learned to have hope when in direst need, and to remember the lessons of misery while in the midst of wealth.

I have always striven to make the best out of any situation, and having many strong interests has helped in these attempts.

Most rewarding, however, has been the artistic creativity that has accompanied me like a guiding thread throughout my life. I have learned that I have brought happiness to people around the world with my creative work, and that is really the greatest satisfaction one can experience in life.

First Experiments
1927

As if awakening from a dream, I leaned back and looked at what my hands had created: an entire playdough menagerie—dogs, birds, an elephant, a rabbit and small, almost-human figurines. Everything was still a little rough, but one could distinguish what it was supposed to be. A happy feeling flowed through me; I had created something that had not existed before.

Only slowly did I realize that the sun was warming my back, that the birds in the two large fir trees in front of the house were singing and that Maria was scolding me because I would get a cold from sitting on the floor, and because I was supposed to wash my hands. Maria was our nanny and I liked her a lot. My mother traveled quite a bit, and so I went to Maria with my problems—and there were a lot of them. In most cases Maria showed an understanding for all the small and great worries that seemed to occupy the mind of a child like me, except she was so finicky when it came to cleanliness.

Yesterday I had celebrated my fifth birthday, and the entire family had been there. There had been cake, hot chocolate and whipped cream, and I had received many gifts. Mother gave me the playdough, which was the greatest present, as I was never bored of working with it. One could always create something new and different. These figurines in front of me were my first ones, and I wanted to preserve them so I could show them to my mother.

My mother was an artist in her own right, because she painted large pictures. Our entire house was filled with them; her oil paintings were even hanging in the stairwell. Adults said that she made copies of famous masters, and all of her acquaintances were full of praise for her work—probably because they hoped they might receive a painting as a gift!

Personally, I liked the painting with the tired horses and the coachman who was lighting a lantern. It was hanging in the living room above the sofa, and I sneaked in there quite often and admired it at length. I also liked the other pictures very much, but somehow the tired horses in the reddish glow of the lantern affected me the most.

While on her most recent journey, Mom had sent me a postcard. On it were marble figures by a famous sculptor. His name was Michelangelo, and he lived many centuries ago in far-away Italy. These figures in marble made a deep impression on me. Sometimes I dreamed about becoming a famous artist whose works were still admired after so many years, like Michelangelo.

But now, working in playdough, I had not been dreaming, but had actually created something myself. Filled with pride, I showed and explained to Maria the individual figurines I had made. But this time she did not show much understanding, she only saw my dirty hands, the oncoming sniffles and the many, multicolored crumbs scattered on the floor all around me, which would be ground into the carpet. And "My Lady," as she called my mother, would not be very happy with that.

However, Maria was wrong about that one thing. When my mother came to see me in the afternoon, my hands were clean, and the crumbs had been picked up. Only the menagerie was standing there, all in a row, one figurine next to the other. "You did a beautiful job," she said with admiration, and inspected each figurine very closely. Then she tenderly stroked my hair (I had long blond locks at the time) and encouraged me to add more figurines to the menagerie. There were, after all, many, many more animals.

"Keep on going with your work," Mom said, "but put a newspaper underneath it, so that Maria will not have to pick up all the crumbs."

Daydreaming
Winter 1928

It was a great moment for me: the king with the glittering crown on his head was sitting majestically on his gem-studded throne. At his side was the beautiful queen in a lovely, flowing gown. Both of them looked graciously down on me. I was standing directly in front of the throne in the great, festively decorated hall filled with many people in their finest garments. At the portal and on both sides of the throne stood guards in their ornate uniforms with their spears.

The king had graciously presented me with a box, the reward for the work I had done. Then he said to me, smiling: "You have fulfilled a lifelong dream of mine in creating this massive monument as an eternal memorial to my gallant father." Everyone in the great hall applauded, and I had a feeling that can hardly be described—as if I was lifted up and floated above the people gathered here. Suddenly I crashed down and awoke: I had had a dream! I had been dreaming in broad daylight! In front of me I saw a fallen horse with an imposing figure on it: a king with sword and crown, shaped out of plastiline as well as I could do it—and then my fantasy bolted.

I had such dreams frequently. In my thoughts I imagined an entire story, forgot my surroundings and experienced these dreams almost as if they were reality. Most often I was the hero, or a famous man in these dreams, and the people were cheering me. I imagine most boys, and probably girls, too, experience such dreams, but very few realize their dreams.

A few days later I received another postcard from my mother, who was traveling quite frequently now. This card was from Florence, and showed Morning Dawn by Michelangelo. This marble figure impressed me very much, and I looked at it again and again. Passing by, Maria inquired, "Are you dreaming again?" In the evening, when my father came home, I asked him about Michelangelo. "Michelangelo Buonarroti was one of the greatest sculptors who ever lived," he explained to me. "His creations, chiseled out of marble, are of immortal beauty. If you should ever go to Italy in your life, you will be able to admire many of his works." He told me a lot more about this great artist who lived four hundred years ago, and gave me a book in which many of his works were pictured. I was deeply impressed, and finally said, "I want to become a great artist myself, and want to create sculptures that will be admired by all men."

My father responded that many men would like to become famous artists but that very, very few succeed in being famous during their lifetime. Then he told me the story of the painter Van Gogh who was a pauper all his life. Only many years after his death did he become famous, and he did not benefit from the fame.

"You will manage our factories later on, as I am doing now," my father told me. "You can be an artist on the side; at least you won't starve this way." My father lived to see that I did not starve as an artist, and that I even gained a little fame in my lifetime. He was very proud of me and only regretted that my mother had not lived long enough to witness my success. With the inborn instincts of a mother, she always maintained that I would someday be a great artist.

Curiosity
Spring 1929

My sister Inge screamed so loudly that it reverberated throughout the house. "My doll, my beautiful new doll, Gerhard has ruined my doll!" When Inge screamed, the noise was so terrible everybody in the house came running—it sounded like she was impaled on a spear. This time was no exception. I saw disaster heading my way. My father could get very angry when something happened to "his" daughter, so I resigned myself to the whipping that would follow. It made no sense to deny my misdeed, since this was the third doll I had examined, and for that purpose I had to cut the belly open. How else could I get to the source of the funny voice inside the doll, which always said "mama?" It was only my quest for exploration, not a desire to upset my sister, that caused me to grab a kitchen knife and slit the body of the doll at approximately the spot from which the voice came.

For her birthday, Inge had received a new doll that was completely different from its predecessors. The earlier dolls had been made out of fabric, and stuffed with some kind of excelsior. Their heads, hands and feet were made out of a heavy porcelain, and nicely painted, too. In these dolls it had not been difficult to reach the voice box that was imbedded in the excelsior. But this new doll was made entirely—head, hands and feet, too—from a different, hard material that one could press in slightly. I later learned that this material was celluloid. It could easily be cut, and soon I had held the coveted voice box in my hand. Inside the box was something like an accordion, with a weight attached. When the doll was put down, the weight pressed on this accordion-like gadget, and made it produce a sound like "mama."

Now I knew how the sound worked, and it simply could not be helped that the doll had been slightly damaged in the process. My curiosity satisfied, I had pulled the doll's dress back down over her body, and placed her in her cradle. But Inge had discovered the damage, and I had to face the consequences of my probing research. I could hear the energetic footsteps of my father approaching. "Gerhard, come here immediately!" Hiding was senseless, and so fate took its course. After all, a nosy boy had to put up with punishment.

Berlin

Autumn 1931

We moved to Berlin! I had only known this large city from previous visits to my Uncle Karl in Berlin-Steglitz. Uncle Karl was a physician— an internist—and had many interesting things in his examination room. I was most fascinated by the large Roentgen (x-ray) machine, which took up almost the entire space of one room, and with which one could see the insides of patients. After office hours, Uncle Karl would show me how this machine worked. Wearing heavy aprons to shield our bodies from the x-rays, we would wait in the darkened room for our eyes to grow accustomed to the darkness. Then Uncle Karl would switch on the machine, and it would hum and crackle ominously. I was allowed to place my arm on the white area, and then I could see, in a mysterious green light, all the bones in my hand.

I also was allowed to watch in his laboratory how his assistants performed blood tests and many other tasks. His lab, filled with ampules, glass tubes and bubbling cylinders, seemed to me to be an alchemist's kitchen. Now we had moved to Berlin, and I thought I would probably be able to visit Uncle Karl more often.

But there were a lot of other things to see in Berlin as well. The city's zoo was one of the largest in the world. One could spend hours there observing the animals. The aquarium made a particularly deep impression on me. In later years I spent many Sundays there, sketching and painting all the animals to which I took a special liking. On Sundays we also visited the museums. The Ethnological Museum and the Pergamon Museum impressed me the most. Then, I was introduced to theater and music, and saw and heard Eroica under the direction of Furtwaengler, and The Flying Dutch Man in the German Opera House. So, in Berlin, new worlds opened for me, and the country boy with his limited horizons became, in the course of time, a world-wise city boy, always on the lookout for new and interesting things.

It was the beginning of the 1930s, a time of great unrest in Berlin. Economic depression and political strife were daily headlines in the newspapers. It was common to find yourself in a dangerous situation. Once when we were shopping, we heard gunshots nearby. My father pulled my sister and me into the hallway of the nearest building, where we were relatively safe. Once inside, we again heard shots and screams. It was only with the greatest effort that my father was able to restrain me from running outside to see what was going on.

In the beginning we lived in the suburb of Tempelhof, not far from the airport. The airplanes, most of them the legendary JU 52's, regularly flew over our house at such low altitude, and with such indescribable noise, that our windows would rattle. So, after a short time, we moved again, this time to Treptow. There our house was very close to the Plaenter woods and the Spree river, which flows through Berlin, was not far. For my sister and myself it was paradise: on one side, the garden and on the other, the woods. And, there was no noise here. The tram stop was only a few minutes from our house, and by tram, the trip to the subway station was only ten minutes long. However it took almost half an hour to get there by foot. By transferring only once, one could be in the center of Berlin in about half an hour.

One day, while strolling in a nearby park, I noticed an unusual building; from a distance it appeared to be a long house with a flat roof and a gigantic pipe on the roof. As I neared the building, I could make out a sign on it that read Treptower Observatory.

My curiosity was aroused, and a few days later I went inside the observatory and noticed a large dome on top of it. The big "pipe" I had seen turned out to be the longest telescope in the world—twenty-one meters long (over 60 feet). As I was looking around the somewhat-darkened waiting room, which was decorated with astronomical displays, an older, distinguished-looking man approached, and asked if he could help me. This was my first encounter with old Mr. Archenholt, builder of the huge telescope and founder of the observatory at the Berlin World Fair in 1898. Mr. Archenholt was also a friend of

Albert Einstein, who publicly spoke about his theory of relativity in this building. Mr. Archenholt apparently took a liking to my child-like curiosity, and showed me the wonders of the cosmos, allowing me to look through the large telescope, and kindling in me the interest for astronomy that in later years developed into a serious study.

Playing in the Sand
Summer 1932

It was a wonderful, warm summer day. The blue waters of the Wannsee competed with the blue of the sky, and the white sails on the water were like reflections of the white clouds that sailed along the sky. The people here had fled metropolitan Berlin, and were enjoying themselves on the white sand of the shore. Some were tanning themselves, and seemed to doze, others were watching those who sprayed each other with water. Still others, more daring, swam out into the lake until the shrill whistle of the lifeguard called them back.

I did not notice any of this; I was busy scraping sand together, especially the sand deeper down, as it was moister and held together better. I was hard at work, toting sand, and starting to shape an arm here, a leg there, with grave concentration. I modeled the head with the greatest of care, because I wanted to create a pretty face. Thus I modeled out of the shapeless pile of sand a human being: a life-size woman at rest. It wasn't until I stood up to survey my creation that I noticed a small crowd around me. They were admiring the little tyke who had shaped such a large figure out of sand. "You, little fellow, are a real artist," remarked a motherly-looking woman, and a fat man commented, "Boy, is she skinny. My wife is a lot heftier." There were many comments about my work, most of an admiring nature. I stood there, very proud of myself, and felt that my model in the sand was very well done. Of course, it was no masterpiece, but for a ten-year-old, it was not bad at all.

Suddenly, two large boys who had been part of the crowd jumped forward and smashed the figure with their feet, laughing and joking as they performed their destructive task. They stopped only when some adults chased them away. But it was too late. Where my "sand lady" had lain just a few moments ago, there was nothing but a pile of shapeless sand. Saddened and angry, I stood with tears in my eyes. I paid no attention to the consoling words of the people around me. Only after considerable time had passed did I notice that I was standing alone at the wreckage of my creation, and I, too, slowly slipped away.

The Torchlight Parade
January 30, 1933

It was a fascinating, eerie spectacle we were witnessing: like a giant glowing centipede, the torchlight parade of the storm troopers in their brown shirts wound through the Brandenburg Gate in Berlin. My parents, sister and I were among the thousands of spectators on the Avenue Unter den Linden, Berlin's most prestigious street, and we watched the brown columns passing by, waving their swastika flags and singing provocative songs. Their heavy jackboots beat upon the pavement and resounded from the buildings. Each of the storm troopers raised his torch as a blazing token of victory. Hitler had managed to take power of Germany and by this torchlight parade he was demonstrating that he intended to use it. Many of the Berliners lining the parade route were cheering wildly for the marchers, since they hoped for an improvement of their often desperate conditions under the new Hitler regime.

The worldwide depression had brought unemployment and poverty to an extent never before experienced. The democratic parties and factions, in their indecisiveness, broke into many splinter factions and finally succumbed to the reactionary forces that had their roots in the fallen Imperial Empire. It was an easy task for the Nazis, with their demagogic and political ploys, to take advantage of the weaknesses of their political opponents. But when arguments failed to produce the desired result, storm troopers helped to achieve it by way of terror. Now Hitler was chancellor of Germany, and he promised the German population that they would not recognize their country ten years from now. It took twelve years before he could keep his promise—but it happened in a way, and with a destruction of such dimension, that nobody could have imagined.

Among the many spectators on this night were some who witnessed the spectacle of power with mixed feelings. One of these was my father, who had a thorough knowledge of German history and was well-informed about the new power-brokers and their intentions. He was in a very somber mood, and as we traveled home on the subway, he remarked: "Let us hope that Hitler will not stay in power for too long, because it will inevitably lead to another war." We children knew from books that war was something terrible, but there is a big difference between reading about war and experiencing it. The perspicacity of my father's assessment was borne out many years later, when Hitler gave his lust for conquest free rein and started the second world war. But my father had no inkling at this time that such extensive persecutions and genocide, ordered by those in power, could happen in a civilized, middle-European country. Nor could he foresee that he would be imprisoned like a criminal in a forced-labor camp for refusing to divorce his spouse, who was of Jewish ancestry.

The beginning of tragedy and misery that Hitler's regime brought upon millions of human beings was this torchlight parade through the Brandenburg gate in Berlin. The causes, however, were to be found in the power struggle and the intolerance of a narrow-minded nationalism, which had its roots in the nineteenth century. While antisemitism was not invented by Hitler, it was conducted by him in total disregard of human dignity, and nearly complete annihilation of the Jews.

A Night of Despair
November 1935

The smell of gas was already very strong. My sister and I were sitting at the open window and looking out into the dark night. "Let's wait a little longer, they probably aren't asleep yet," I whispered to Inge. Only a few hours ago we had found out, quite by accident, what our parents had planned. They had been sitting in the living room and thought that we were already asleep. But I had had to go out again, and passed the living room, the door to which was not completely closed. I heard sobbing, and nervous conversation.

Since our last factory had closed, things had gone downhill rapidly. We had no money left. All the furniture had been impounded, and even the grocer refused to let us buy on credit. My father had suffered a nervous breakdown, and my mother couldn't cope any longer. Filled with hopelessness and despair, my parents had planned that tonight, after we children were asleep, they would open the gas burners on the stove and close the windows. We would never see another morning, and our troubles would be over.

As soon as I heard this I woke up my sister and told her. We had to stop this, and planned to turn off the gas burners as soon as our parents were asleep.

Now it seemed the time for action had come. We pressed handkerchiefs to our mouths, and sneaked past our parents' open bedroom door into the kitchen. Inge held the flashlight while I turned off the main burner. Then we silently opened the windows and let

14

fresh air stream in. Only then did we sigh in relief—we had barely escaped death.

The next morning our parents appeared somewhat embarrassed, but never mentioned a word about the events of the night. Rays of sunlight shone in through the window, and the world seemed happier than it had the past night.

My parents faced our difficulties with a new spirit and courage. My mother found a position with the Electrolux company in advertising and sales. The daughter of wealthy parents, who had never worked a day in her life, she went from house to house demonstrating vacuum cleaners. She turned out to be very successful, and was able to land my father a job with the same company as a sales representative. They were working together, and soon things began to improve. We paid off our debts, and over the years we acquired a level of modest wealth. Only many years later did we discuss with our parents that fateful night in which we decided between life and death.

A Revelation
Summer 1937

We had never talked about it before because it had not been a problem. Now we were sitting around the big table in our living room: my parents, my sister and I. My parents looked worried, and they revealed why. We were a "non-Aryan" family, because my mother was of Jewish descent. She had converted to Catholicism before she married my father, but this did not change the fact that she had been born a Jew.

The term "non-Aryan" had not existed before this time, at least not in an official sense. Before the Nazis came to power, the Jews were not well-liked by right-wing Germans, but at least they were tolerated. People admired the intelligence of the Jews, and their cultural talents. It had been the Jews who set the pace, especially in the arts, during the "Golden Twenties" following World War I.

The Nazis had come to power with the aid of an economic crisis and the support of the middle-of-the-road parties, and with financing by the large industrial syndicates. Those who had read Hitler's book, *Mein Kampf*—and my father was one of those few—feared for the future. Through a very efficient propaganda campaign, the Nazis promised the starving Germans a rosy future. Hitler succeeded in getting the jobless masses off the streets by well-planned measures such as the labor service and the revitalization of the armaments industry. Ostentatious parades, flag-waving, fanfare and national slogans diverted the public's attention from what was really going on in the background: persecution, incarceration, deportation and even

16

murder of those who criticized or opposed the new regime. As for the miserable situation of the past few years in Germany, it was easy to find scapegoats to blame: the Jews, towards whom Hitler harbored a deep and personal hatred. So began a well-calculated, cruel genocide, the likes of which the world had never seen. At the time, we anticipated hardships, but we had no inkling of the heinous deeds of which the citizens of a nation with such high cultural standards were capable.

My father came from an old family of Prussian government servants, which had served the country under Frederick the Great. He had been a reserve officer of the "green Hussars" in our home state of Silesia, and had been decorated with the Iron Cross in World War I. While a student at the universities of Breslau and Berlin, he had belonged to a fraternity. He fell in love with the daughter of a neighbor, a Jewish owner of a textile factory, and they were married right after the war. My father continued his studies, but after the unexpected death of his father-in-law, he was forced to take over the management of the textile plants.

My father, reflecting on his past, finally said, "There is nothing they can do to us. I have always been a good German citizen, fought for the country, and never ran afoul of the law. Maybe things will not be so bad after all, and probably the Nazis will not stay in power very long." But, while the following years were relatively quiet and peaceful, my father was overly optimistic.

My father was employed by Electrolux, a Swedish company, first as a salesman and later in a management position. The influence of the Nazis was limited when it came to a foreign company; in fact, they showed greater tolerance. But then the so-called "Nuremberg" laws were enacted, which prohibited me from attending high school.

At this time, my mother's sister emigrated with her family to New Zealand. Before they left, my uncle had a serious talk with my father, and urged him to follow suit, and leave this inhospitable country. But my father was fond of Germany. What's more, he had no money to emigrate and build a new life in New Zealand.

Many of our Jewish relatives also emigrated, some of them in time to escape persecution, some of them very late. Another relative of my mother's who emigrated to New Zealand had been able to take his car along. He had devised a clever deception for taking his wealth: he had all the chrome trimmings on his old car replaced with platinum. My Uncle Karl, who had married my mother's second sister and had a flourishing medical practice in Berlin did not leave until after Kristallnacht in November 1938, which marked the escalation of the persecution of the Jews. I still have the medical instruments Uncle Karl used in the combat zone during World War I.

My family remained in Germany, and found ourselves exposed to more and more harassment and persecution. At times, we were forced to resort to sly deception in order to save our lives, and were able to survive this terrible period only through enormous luck, determination and a strong will to live.

Max and Moritz

Summer 1938

My heart was beating excitedly, for that was not a dog I had on the end of the leash—I was walking a full-grown dragon! With each plodding step of the Komodo-Waran's, the sharp claws of this giant lizard made a strange, almost whirring noise on the tile floor. At the same time, with each turn of his head, the reptile's forked tongue shot out of his closed mouth. It took some time to accept that I was not dreaming, but was really leading a live dragon on a leash. I finally dared to call him by his name: Moritz. He raised his head towards me, and looked at me quizzically with his prehistoric eyes. On my left plodded Max, the second of these rare lizards, which can only be found on the island of Komodo in Indonesia. Max was led by the zoo keeper on his daily walk in the aquarium of the Berlin Zoo. This zoo keeper had been caring for these giant Warans for many years.

We walked along the long hall adjacent to the aquarium on this very early Sunday morning, long before the zoo opened to the public, so that the animals could get their daily exercise. They hardly moved at all during the day when they were confined to their climate-controlled enclosure, and visitors had to watch for long hours before one of the lizards even stirred.

I had always been very interested in reptiles in their prehistoric atmosphere, and during my strolls I had often observed lizards sunning themselves on rocks, and catching insects. I was most fascinated, however, by dinosaurs, extinct for so many millions of years, and read many books written about these inhabitants of our globe in prehis-

19

toric times. With the greatest of interest, I followed the discovery and excavation of skeletons, the painstaking restoration work and their exhibits in museums. Not all of these creatures were large, but some of them had developed into the largest type of animal ever to inhabit this earth. They existed long before mankind, and had ruled the land, the water and the air long before we came along. I had often dreamed about dinosaurs, and even fought duels with them—in a dream all this is possible!

After we moved to Berlin I often visited not only the zoo, but also the aquarium, at that time the largest in the world. There I spotted the Komodo-Warans, Max and Moritz, for the first time. From my very first glimpse I was fascinated by them, mainly by their similarity to the extinct dinosaurs, and spent many many hours watching them in their glass-enclosed environment. I made a number of sketches of this pair. (Unfortunately, these were lost in Berlin during the war years.) One day the zoo keeper in charge of these creatures approached me. His name was Weber, and he had observed how many hours I had spent observing and sketching these two animals. We talked about the Warans and I tried to learn as much as possible about their origin and habits. Then, he made a fascinating offer: If I came to a side entrance early the following Sunday, two hours before the aquarium opened, he would wait for me and let me in. I would have a chance to lead one of these giant lizards on a leash on their morning walk. He assured me that both of them were docile, since they were cared for and well-fed, and that he was not worried as long as I followed his instructions. I was thrilled, immediately accepted, and spent the next few days in eager anticipation.

On Sunday, long before the appointed time, I stood at the side entrance. I had come by subway and streetcar through the deserted city, worried about getting to my destination on time. Finally the gate opened, and a smiling Mr. Weber greeted me with the words: "I bet you have been waiting here a while." He must have sensed my feverish anticipation. We went along the long corridors and stairways to the Waran enclosure. When he opened the door, the two giant lizards just glanced at us, but they came alive when he called their names. Then I had to talk to them so that they would get used to me. I was so excited that at first I didn't know what to say, but then I decided to talk to them like I talked to our dachshund at home. It seemed like a dream. I pinched my arm. It hurt, and that meant I really was in the

Waran enclosure! Mr. Weber attached strong leashes to Max and then to Moritz, and the morning stroll began.

We marched down the hallways, at first hesitantly and slowly, but soon picking up the pace. "They know that at the end of the walk they will receive their meat ration, or they would not go along so willingly," Mr. Weber explained. After about half an hour, we returned to their enclosure, and I watched them being fed. When Mr. Weber tossed them their meat, they probed it at first with their forked tongues before they sank their claws into it and tore off great chunks which they swallowed in one piece. I could hardly tear myself away from Max and Moritz but opening time had arrived and it was time for me to leave. I thanked the care-taker for this exciting experience before going on my way home. Unfortunately, I never saw Mr. Weber again. When I inquired about him I was told that he had been drafted into the armed forces. War was imminent and reservists everywhere in Germany were called up. So this morning walk remained a one-time encounter, one which I will remember for the rest of my life.

At the Reimann Institute

October 1940

An atmosphere of high tension prevailed in the classroom, broken only by the scratching of the charcoal pen, and an occasional sigh from a student. The model was sitting on an elevated pedestal in the center, where she could be seen by all the students. The instructor went from student to student, giving advice or correcting the drawing. This is how I remember the drawing of my first nude, a lesson at the Institute of Art and Work—the famous Reimann Institute. Reimann, like many contemporary members of the art world during the 1920s, was a Jew. He had founded and managed this prestigious school himself until the Nazis took it away from him. Reimann had then emigrated, and his school was taken over by the city of Berlin, and given a new name. However, it always remained the "Reimann Institute" and the majority of the instructors, and even the students, were individualists who criticized, and often opposed, the Nazis. My sister Inge and I had enrolled in evening classes. I studied drawing and sculpting; Inge attended the painting class.

Time went by quickly. We had ten-minute sessions, then the model changed position. It required great concentration to comprehend the various positions and proportions in such a short time, and to put them down on paper.

During the short breaks, the halls and stairways were crowded with young people engaged in discussion while chewing their sandwiches. Most of them rushed here after a long day at work, in order to study the various arts. Master classes were offered in all aspects of art; everything from life drawing, graphics, painting and sculpting to film direction and fashion photography was taught at this unique institute. For me it was inspiring to study as part of this community of enthusiastic young people. There were only about a dozen students in Professor Melzer's sculpting class, most of them girls, since most of the boys of this age had been drafted into the armed forces. The war was in its second year, and seeing a young man without a uniform was a rarity.

For my first project in the sculpting class I had chosen to create the Three Graces in the form of a relief. Professor Melzer smiled benevolently when he saw my effort; he knew I had been too ambitious with this particular project. But he gave me a free hand, only correcting where absolutely necessary. Portrait busts and torsos were my next projects. Time flew, and at the end of the lesson we packed our clay models in damp cloths, wrapped them in oil-soaked paper and covered them with large buckets in order to keep them from drying out. I picked up my sister from the painting class, and we hurried home before an air-raid alarm might keep us from getting there. We had to transfer twice, from the underground railroad to the metro and finally to a street car. It was almost eleven o'clock by the time we got home.

Since tonight was a clear and bright evening, I got off the street car two stations before my usual stop, and went to the Treptower Observatory. I had become a member of the astronomical society many years earlier, and had a special interest in the planets and space travel, which at that time existed only in theory. The society was a group of very enthusiastic amateur astronomers, all of us young people, but we did a lot of professional work, together with professional astronomers, in the study of planets and the sun. At the observatory there were excellent instruments, experimental rooms, a library and an auditorium for our use. I spent many a night with the telescope, observing and charting Jupiter, Mars, the moon and the sun. We had numerous discussions about space travel in the future, and as a member of the society for interstellar space research I met important researchers such as Hermann Oberth and Werner von Braun, who laid the foundation for today's space travel. We also met with other outstanding scientists such as Baron von Ardenne, Dr. Gramatzki and Dr. Weber, and spent marvelous hours together. Thus

we became some of the first people to view molecules, which had been
made visible in Baron von Ardenne's electron-microscope.

I am still amazed today when I think of how little sleep I could
get by with at that time. Very often it was not more than three to four
hours a night, and even less as the bombing of Berlin escalated. This
was an unforgettable period of my life, a period of tensions and dan-
gers during which we were young and passionately involved in art and
science.

I am still in touch with many of my friends from that era, and we
continue to meet from time to time in Berlin or in the United States.
Almost all of them have remained loyal to science; only I took a different road, and followed the direction of my studies at the Reimann
Institute. I was very happy there, and deep down I hoped to find my
way as an artist, although I had no idea how, when or where I would
do this. The war was raging, but we knew that Germany could not
win it, and my small hopes for an artistic career were kindled only by
the thought of what might happen after the war ended.

Optical Experiments
Summer 1943

The shavings were swirling through the air, and glittered brightly when a ray of sunlight caught them. I was standing at the lathe, shaping a capsule out of shiny brass. It was going to be a special gauge for the artillery. By using such an instrument, a gunner could avoid hitting the protective gun emplacement. Before me I had the blueprint "Papa Kollmorgen" had given me. Those close to him among his staff called him Papa Kollmorgen because he was like a good father to us. I cannot remember ever hearing a harsh or angry word from him. Even though I was only an apprentice, he took me into his experimental unit, where I developed new optical instruments under his guidance. I worked practically independently, and had to report only to Papa Kollmorgen, much to the envy of my colleagues.

It was more than two years now that I had been employed as an apprentice at this factory for special optical instruments. The training in this profession enabled me to build telescopes and microscopes by myself, which I needed for my hobbies of astronomy and microscopy. But most important, due to this very specialized training, I was never drafted into the German Wehrmacht or other war-related organizations. Papa Kollmorgen had excellent connections to the highest staffs of the German army and only his protection enabled my family and me to survive the war without harm. I shall always remember his protective care with deep gratitude.

At this time I worked up to seventy-two hours a week with insufficient rations. After working, I would proceed with my studies at the

Reimann Institute and after class, on clear nights, I would go to the telescope at the Treptower Observatory and draw planetary sketches.

My few remaining hours of sleep and rest were more and more often interrupted by air-raid sirens, and the falling of bombs and other incendiary devices on Berlin. After each air raid I would go into the attic to search for possible incendiary bombs. My mother had knitted a pair of asbestos mittens for me, and with these I was able to grab the incendiary bombs and toss them into the garden through an open window.

These were tough times, but I would not have wanted to miss them; my will to live was of an intensity I rarely experienced in later years. It was only our hope that the Nazi regime would collapse with the inevitable end of the war that gave us all the strength to pull through these difficult years.

In April 1944, the Kollmorgen company suffered irreparable damage from an air raid, and the staff and machinery were transferred to Coburg. This is how I came to the city of Coburg. Compared to life in Berlin, Coburg was paradise! It was a city without any war damage, which was never bombed—presumably because of the family ties between the Dukes of Coburg and the British Royal Family. (Prince Albert, husband of Queen Victoria, was a Duke of Coburg.)

In Coburg the Kollmorgen Company was established in the building of a former flag factory. The machinery was set up and in only a few weeks we were in full production again. My job was now to test and make final adjustments of the instruments before they were handed over to the purchasing officer from the army. One of the requirements of my job was to travel to Berlin every so often, and this gave me a chance to visit my family. But a young man not in army uniform was conspicuous, and often drew the attention of the military police. Once when I was sitting in the train compartment and drawing my fellow travelers (mostly older people and soldiers) in a little sketchbook I always carried with me, the compartment door was suddenly jerked open and two military policemen roared, "ID papers!" One of the two spotted me in my civilian clothes and, with a sneer on his face, proclaimed, "Aha, here we have one of these draft dodgers!" Then he drew himself up to his imposing height, and demanded to know why I was not in the armed forces.

I was well-prepared for this question. With a gracious smile, I pulled a letter from my jacket and held it out to him. After only a brief scanning of the letter, he underwent a sudden change of attitude. A moment ago he had been an imposing policeman, now he was the picture of servitude. He stammered: "Sorry, I didn't mean it that way," and begged me not to report him for his rudeness.

I had obtained this "miracle" letter through Papa Kollmorgen. It came from our forces' Supreme Headquarters, and was signed by a general. The letter advised all military authorities to be of assistance to me in any way possible. Saluting stiffly and clicking their heels, these two grumpy fellows departed, forgetting to check the papers of my fellow travelers. A sigh of relief went through the compartment, coupled with looks of curiosity towards me. Finally, an older gentleman sitting across from me inquired what could be the contents of the letter that caused such a sudden change in the attitude of the military police. I explained, satisfying the curiosity of most of my companions. Only one elderly woman sadly said: "How unfair this war is! My son was taken prisoner by the Russians in Stalingrad, and I do not know if I will ever see him again." I could only be silent in response.

Coburg
January 1945

The stars were shining and glittering on this cold clear winter night. The town looked like something in a fairy tale; fresh snow-covered houses and streets, the lanterns had white caps, and here and there was the small glow of a light. One could almost forget that there was a war going on, a war that had brought great misery and sorrow to many, but the end of which was near at hand. We walked alongside each other, pulling the sled that held our suitcases. We had met only a few minutes before. I had come from Berlin by train, and was heading home with my heavy suitcase, tired from the long journey, when I heard the snow crackle behind me. Then a very pleasant voice said: "I believe we are going in the same direction; why don't you put your suitcase on my sled?" I turned to see the slender figure of a girl pulling a sled. She smiled at me, and that was the beginning of my first great love.

After a few strides in silence, she introduced herself. I should have been the one to introduce myself to her, but I was just too shy. Her name was Lia, and she was a soprano at our local opera house. Then I remembered that I had seen and heard her several times at the opera house, which was now closed due to lack of coal. Lia was very charming, and knew how to conquer my shyness—which was especially evident in relationships with the female sex. Soon we were engaged in animated conversation as we pulled the sled through the snow-covered streets. We did not live very far from each other, and I finally got up enough courage to ask her for a date, to which she

28

agreed immediately. We both felt lonesome in these troubled times, and saw each other whenever possible. At first we would meet in a restaurant, then later in her or my apartment. We talked about everything, philosophizing about God and the world, and while my affection for her grew, I didn't dare to declare my love.

One night I awoke from a terrible nightmare. Our house in Berlin had been hit by a bomb and had caved in, burying my mother and my sister. Immediately I was wide awake, and knew that something terrible had happened. My father had been arrested by the Gestapo several months ago, and was confined to a labor camp, for refusing to divorce my Jewish mother. My sister was forced to work as a seamstress in a factory that made parachutes, and my mother was afraid to venture out into the street alone. We made our neighbors believe that she was visiting relatives. The situation went from bad to worse, the Nazis were getting more apprehensive and capable of misdeeds of any kind. Within minutes I had worked out a plan—I had to go to Berlin immediately. I was the only one in our family who could still travel without restrictions.

A few hours later I was sitting in the train carrying me to Berlin. Papa Kollmorgen had granted me emergency leave and arranged for everything. He also provided me with a legitimate purchase order for the acquisition of materials for our plant, and I carried with me the letter from Supreme Headquarters as protection against the military police. Just in case, I toted along a small revolver.

When the train approached the vicinity of the LEUNA chemical works, the air-raid sirens sounded in their usual wail. We were being strafed by fighter planes and threw ourselves on the floor. The train was now progressing very slowly. Suddenly railroad police appeared, and announced that all passengers had to leave the train in Jueterbog, a distant suburb of Berlin. Nobody was allowed to enter the capital. The Russian army had encircled Berlin almost completely; only to the south was there a gap through which trains still could pass. But I had to go to Berlin no matter what! I showed my precious papers to the official, who informed me that there would be no exceptions to this order.

When we arrived in Jueterbog, it was already dark. Everybody left the train. I, however, had formed a plan. I crawled up on the upper luggage net and covered myself with my coat. I held my small revolver in my hand and hoped that the railroad police, who surely would return for a final inspection, would just shine their flashlights on the lower seats, and not notice me above them. After a long wait I heard steps and the slamming of compartment doors: the tension was unbearable! Finally a beam of light appeared at the door, which opened just a crack. I held my breath and tightened my grip on the revolver. I heard a grouchy voice mutter, "nothing here," the door slammed shut and the steps grew fainter. I breathed a sigh of relief—for the time being I was safe. But I was not in Berlin yet. I remained in my uncomfortable hiding place and waited until the train started moving ever so slowly. Only then did I dare come down from my perch and look outside. The window panes had been blown out a long time ago, and the windows were boarded up with wooden slats. I was able to see a little through a wider crack in the slats. The train rolled very slowly through the southern suburbs of Berlin. An acrid smell permeated the air, and the thunder of cannon fire could be heard in the distance. After a long time, and a lot of shunting over various tracks, the train finally stopped. The locomotive was disconnected. I had arrived at my destination!

I jumped down onto the tracks and darted across the rails of a dark freight station. After a ride on the still-functioning subway, I walked through streets covered with rubble. This was truly an inferno. The harsh stench of smoke prickled my nose. Many houses were burning and in the distance one could hear the cannon fire of the approaching Russians. People, their faces reflecting utter hopelessness, ran aimlessly through the streets, interspersed with small groups of young soldiers . Only now did I, who came from a small and peaceful town in the country, realize the extent of insanity to which this war had escalated. This once-beautiful metropolis was buried in rubble and ashes, and many people died an agonizing death, just because Hitler was too stubborn to accept that the war was lost.

At dawn I finally reached our house and saw that my nightmare had become a reality. A heavy bomb had landed in our garden and torn a tremendous crater in the earth. The blast of the explosion had forced all the inside walls to cave in, and all was chaos—debris, doors torn from their hinges, over-turned furniture. My mother and sister, their faces strained from lack of sleep, were trying to create some kind of order from this mess. Thankfully, they were alive and unharmed. Their tired eyes lit up when they spotted me, and we fell into each others' arms. I told them: "You have to get out of here. You are going to Coburg with me!"

"And how are we going to accomplish that?" asked my sister. The air raids and constant threats by the Nazis had made her lethargic and discouraged. After we had cleared out the debris in buckets, and righted the furniture, we had nothing left but a few dishes. Then we nailed cardboard over the windows, as glass was no longer available, rested a few minutes and gathered our thoughts. I had to use a lot of persuasion to shake my mother and sister out of their lethargy and convince them that we should try anything to get away from this inferno. Very soon I came up with a workable plan. Our family physician, who was a close friend of ours, was to attest that Inge was ill, so that any inquiries from her employer would be delayed. Since we would not be able to legally purchase railroad tickets for the two of them, I had to touch up some used tickets of mine to make them look legitimate. In the general chaos, and together with my valid documents, we had a chance! And we did indeed succeed in leaving the beleaguered city with the barest necessities on, literally, the very last train.

In Coburg I found lodging for my mother and Inge at Professor Poertzel's house. Shortly after my transfer to Coburg I had sought connections with the local group of artists and had met Professor Poertzel, who had offered me an empty room in the attic as shelter. With the use of a ladder, this attic room even had a separate entrance. I had moved into this artist's studio, fixed it up and remained there until the war ended. Professor Poertzel and I became very good friends, despite our difference in age. In my spare time I assisted him with his sculpting and learned a great deal from him. When I mentioned to him that I was trying to get my family out of Berlin and bring them to Coburg, he immediately offered them quarters in his large house. At that time he did not know that my mother was Jewish. I was not sure that he would have offered assistance so spontaneously if he had known it.

The End of the War
April 1945

The clanking and grinding noises came closer and closer, shots rang out. It was safer to stay here in the basement as long as the air outside was laced with so much "iron." But we felt an urge to go upstairs and outside to greet our liberators—U.S. troops were entering Coburg and resistance was sporadic. Remnants of Wehrmacht units (consisting mostly of old men and teenagers) were retreating towards the East. The shelling of the town was brief. Shots were coming from the Veste, an old fortress high above the city, until a hit from an American gun set one building afire. Then there was deathly silence. We ran up from the basement and out into the main street. Everywhere people were emerging from basements and foxholes. Then we saw tanks roaring towards us, soldiers with rifles at the ready riding on top. We waved at them and shouted greetings in English.

Suddenly a small boy ventured out into the street, very close to a tank, and waved. The tank stopped, and everyone held their breath. A huge black soldier, sitting close to the turret, reached inside and then stretched out his hand to the little boy. In it he held a chocolate bar. "That's for you," he said in a deep voice. The boy stared wide-eyed at the grinning soldier, then grabbed the chocolate.

The ice was broken. Some people close by applauded, others called out "welcome!" So this was the way the U.S. soldiers behaved—quite differently from what the Nazi propaganda had wanted us to believe. Instead of spearing the little boy with his bayonet, this "black devil" gave him a bar of chocolate! Now other children tore them-

selves loose from their mothers and ran towards the tank to get their
share of candy. The soldier laughingly distributed his goodies until
everybody had a piece, then the tank rumbled on.

So this was the end of the tyranny we had awaited for so long.
Only very slowly did we realize that all danger had passed. We did
not have to hide anymore, no SS or Gestapo could harm us any longer.
We had survived—it was an indescribable feeling! It felt as though
we had been resurrected. This moment restored our self-esteem.
Embracing each other and holding hands, we stood at the curb and
watched the passing tanks. The hum of their motors was the song of
freedom.

But not everyone in Coburg was in a happy mood. Many had a
bad conscience and did not want to admit that they were to blame
for the disaster that had descended on Germany, if only by tolerat-
ing the oppressing laws enacted by the Nazis. (This toleration had its
roots in the German attitude of servitude, which had been nourished
by rulers to centuries.) Thy total war proclaimed by Hitler was followed by a total collapse of a magnitude never before experienced
in Germany's history. Central Europe was a huge pile of rubble with
millions dead, unimaginable suffering, hunger and deportation—all
the legacy of an insane despot.

After this memorable day of liberation, the task of a fresh start
lay ahead. It took only a few days for a military government to be
established in Coburg, and the chaos was slowly replaced by law and
order. But fundamental changes in thinking and in laws were in the
offing, as well as the tremendous task of rebuilding the cities. At the
time it seemed impossible that a model democracy would develop in
this ravaged country, and that it would emerge as one of the richest
countries in this world. Right now, however, we had an immediate
goal: to find living quarters and food! And through all this, we worried about the fate of my father.

Together Again

June 1945

The bell had rung—a very unusual sound for us to hear. For several days we had been living in the house of a Nazi official who had fled. Lieutenant Pelz of the U.S. military government had assigned it to us as living quarters. He had also given us some real coffee, and my mother had baked a cake. I had bartered for the ingredients with some friends of Professor Poertzel in a village outside Coburg.

Now I went to the door to see who had rung the bell, and a shout of joy came from me: "Dad is home!" He looked somewhat strained and tired, but very happy. His arrival meant that he had received my coded message that the family was in Coburg now, and we were all united again. After having some coffee and cake, he took a bath—which he had not had for a long time—and then we sat together until late in the night. I had managed to get a bottle of wine somewhere, and thus we toasted to a new life in peace and freedom.

We had a lot to talk about: our spectacular flight from Berlin, the uncertainty of the past few weeks and, finally, the end of the war. My father related his experiences in the camp, which had been guarded by a French contingent of the SS. The prisoners had been forced to do hard labor for the road construction company of Sager & Woerner in the area of Halle, always under the guard of SS troops. Since my father was somewhat fluent in French, he had been able to strike up a kind of friendship with one of the guards. The guards had grown more and more nervous and tense as the front lines came closer. One evening the guard my father had befriended revealed to him that they would withdraw during the night, but would destroy the camp before leaving, and advised him not to remain in the barracks.

My father talked this over with his fellow prisoners and they decided to seek refuge in an underground trench underneath the barracks. After a long wait, the silence above was broken by shrill commands and bursts of machine-gun fire. Then it was quiet again. When the prisoners finally thought it safe, they emerged to look about. The SS guards were gone; the barracks had been riddled with machine-gun fire. If the prisoners had not taken shelter in the trench, there would not have been many survivors.

Finally U.S. troops arrived and distributed rations and supplies in the camp. A U.S. army officer asked about the nature of this particular camp, and the reasons for the prisoners' incarcerations. My father acted as interpreter, since he was also fluent in English. A few days later, the camp was dissolved, and everyone tried to get home as soon as possible. There was no public transportation, so everybody struck out on foot. I had sent my father a postcard stating that "Aunt Ruth" (Ruth being my mother's middle name) and her daughter had been transferred to Coburg, and he had interpreted it correctly. So he turned southward, and walked more than one hundred and sixty miles, over country roads and through fields, together with another former prisoner, the director of a bank in Sonneberg (a town near Coburg). They had slept in barns and sheds; some farmers had given them food and pointed them towards Coburg. After five days my father finally arrived in Coburg, and learned our new address from Professor Poertzel.

Coburg, like all German cities at that time, was overcrowded with refugees, but since the city had suffered no damage from the war, life soon returned to a somewhat normal pace. After my father had recovered from the rigors of his past few weeks, he applied for a job at U.S. military government headquarters in Coburg, and was immediately given a job in the city administration. Later, when a trustee was needed for a metal factory, also in Coburg, he was offered this job, since he was known to be a qualified and politically reliable man.

As for me, I had artistic ambitions, but did not know quite how to go about achieving them. My friend Lia had formed a private class for English lessons, and it was there that I met the renowned film director Paul Verhoeven, who was to make the movie *Das Kleine Hofkonzert* when the end of the war surprised him. Verhoeven and

his cameraman wanted to go to Munich in order to probe the possi-
bilities of a new start. He had never worked as part of the Nazi propaganda machine, but had only made movies that were family entertainment. He invited me to go to Munich with him, and I agreed
enthusiastically. The American Red Cross requested we find musical
scores for a variety show, and for this purpose we received an old car
from the motor pool.

Making a trip to Munich only a few weeks after the war's end
was a risky undertaking, but after surviving several breakdowns, and
many other problems, we made it. We were able to fill up with gaso-
line at U.S. army installations thanks to our American Red Cross certificate. Very often it was difficult to snake our way through the rubble
of the cities; only the main arteries had been cleared by the legendary Truemmer-Frauen. (Since there were hardly any able-bodied men,
women were assigned to the task of clearing the rubble in major cities.) It took courage and hope for the future to clear the streets of
the huge piles of rubble, knowing that at any moment the remaining
ruins might cave in. Women took the first step in rebuilding what
men had destroyed. They chopped the mortar from the bricks that
were still usable and toted the rest of the rubble to special areas in
handcarts. These are hard tasks in the best circumstances, and the
women worked with half-empty stomachs due to insufficient food
rations.

We inspected the ruins of the Bavarian National Theater; it would
take many years, if not decades, of reconstruction before the curtain
could rise again. The Prinzregenten-Theater was reasonably well-
preserved, and here Paul Verhoeven became the director. I witnessed
many a performance under his direction. Through him I made the
acquaintance of many famous German actors and actresses in theater and movie circles. Yet, even though I was fascinated by all this, I
realized that it could not be my world.

Barters and Transactions
April 1946

Tires squealing, I stopped my "Wanderer Cabric" at the entrance to the U.S. Army Post Exchange. We were dressed smartly, and my sister Inge had even applied the appropriate make-up. With an air of self-confidence, I got out of the car, went around and opened the door for Inge. Then, loaded down with packages, we climbed the steps to the front entrance, which was reserved for U.S. military personnel only. Apparently we made the impression we had hoped. The guards at the door not only did not ask us for identification, but responded to my sloppy salute by opening the door for us! We had cleared that hurdle! We spotted only a handful of civilians among all the uniformed personnel. We took our packages to a valuator, mumbled something in English, and proceeded to unpack our "barter ware": porcelain figures, and a few Hummel figurines, which I had received from Franz Goebel. Hummel figurines were already worth a very high exchange rate, since the U.S. GIs were eager to acquire them.

After we had received our coupons, we used them to buy coffee, cigarettes and chocolates, all of which were unobtainable at any regular store in Germany. Meanwhile, the back doors of the Exchange had been opened for the German civilians, and the masses poured in, loaded down with packages and handbags. We, however, were already finished and left through the front door. Another sloppy salute from me, and the guard opened the car door for Inge.

We had thoroughly practiced this masquerade as American civilians for just one purpose: self-confidence. Both my sister and I had an inferiority complex, probably as a result of constant persecution during the Nazi era. Even now, two years after the war, we were still suffering from it, and it was very difficult to overcome, as well as difficult to cope with.

I had visited the American barter exchange several times in order to trade for rare articles of food. It was the only legal place to acquire coffee, cigarettes (at the time I smoked) and other desirable goods. Most importantly, for each transaction we received an official bill of sales, which had to be shown at police checkpoints. The checkpoints were there to control the flow of black market goods, and if we did not have the papers, our goods would be confiscated. It was impossible at that time to live reasonably well with the official ration coupons, and thus illegal exchanges proliferated. Our worthless German currency had been replaced by the cigarette currency—on the black market everything was quoted only in "cigarette" values.

My father had been able to hire me as the purchasing agent as well as sales manager of the Brose metalworks, which he headed as trustee, because of my commercial and technical training. This was done with the consent of the authority that supervised the transition of Nazi property. My main task was the procurement of raw materials—a very difficult job during this time since such materials could also only be acquired by barter. I designed and constructed a ceramic iron with an unusual quality and an appealing design for those times. This very desirable item opened the doors to commerce officials and related ministries and, in this way, I was able to acquire coal, sheet metal and all the other materials necessary for our production. We were able to hire more and more people, and produce urgently needed goods such as kitchen ranges. The need for basic goods and necessities in war-ravaged Germany was tremendous. From gas-mask containers of Germany army vintage we fashioned watering cans. Ideas were rewarded. But I also constructed electric car-window openers, and we installed the first set in the car of Coburg's military commander. Manually-operated window openers had been an essential part of the production of the Brose company, but were not in great demand at this time, due to the lagging auto industry. Today, Brose is a leading manufacturer in this segment of the industry in Europe.

My car—a Wanderer sport Cabric—made me a very attractive young man for the girls of Coburg, since cars were a rarity in Germany at that time. A number of girls, most of them very beautiful, tried to steer me towards the port of matrimony, and their mothers and aunts did their best to help. I resisted these efforts for a while, but eventually gave in. Hannelore appealed to me very much, and after only a short time we were married—against the will of my parents. But who listens to his parents in a situation like this!

A Merry Jail
June 1946

The jail on Coburg's Leopold Street had never seen such merriment. All night long we drank wine and sang jolly songs, along with the jail attendant. We were three Coburg citizens who had been sent to jail within a short time of each other by a U.S. army patrol, for alleged speeding. All three of us were of the opinion that we were the victims of some mysterious red tape, since none of us had exceeded the speed limit. I knew for sure that I had not, since I had recently replaced my broken fan belt with a rope—and with that kind of makeshift repair, one simply couldn't drive fast. But all of our arguments with the U.S soldiers had gone for naught, and we were arrested and delivered to the jail.

Since we were not "major" criminals, the warden allowed us to spend the time in the waiting room, rather than in individual cells. We sat on rickety chairs; the room was lit only by a dim bulb. Our warden, who seemed to be long past retirement age, reminded me of the jailer Frosch in the operetta *Die Fledermaus* by Johann Strauss. He smoked a pipe with a terrible stench, and drank some undefinable liquid from a tin cup. We three prisoners discussed our situation, and came to the conclusion that at this late hour there was nothing we could do. Probably the next morning we would have a full explanation of the mistakes that led to our arrests. I was allowed to call my father and inform him of our misfortune.

"I still have a case of wine in my car," said the friendly chubby man who had introduced himself as a wine merchant. The third man was owner of a lumberyard. Under the watchful eye of the jailer, we retrieved the case of wine from the car, and opened the first bottle. We managed to find some slightly chipped glasses somewhere, and it was not long before we were in a happy mood. Our old warden joined us—after all, he had to keep his eyes on us—and helped empty the bottles. Someone started to sing, and pretty soon merry tunes emanated from the jail, probably to the astonishment of the citizens who lived nearby. Morning was dawning by the time we had emptied most of the bottles, and we fell asleep on our uncomfortable chairs. Our drinking buddy, the warden, finally woke us and told us that we had been granted freedom. Orders had come from the American military government to release us immediately. In his grumbly voice he thanked us for the good wine and wished us the very best. We departed feeling that our stay in jail had been, after all, quite comfortable and happy.

Several months later I received a package from the United States with many delicacies: coffee, cigarettes, and cans of meat products. A letter was enclosed. It was from a military policeman, who apologized for our arrest and told me the reason for it. He had applied for furlough at that time, and needed a few more "points," which he could only get by making several arrests. With the consent of his colleague, he arrested a few drivers under the pretext of speeding, and thus we three found ourselves in this happy jail. He hoped to make up for the injustice by sending me this package. In my thoughts, I forgave him.

Emigration, and A Wise Decision

September 1947

We embraced once more. Then, with tears in her eyes, yet filled with hope for the future, my sister Inge boarded the vessel anchored at the Columbus Pier in Bremerhaven. A short while later Inge appeared again high in the open promenade, and we had to communicate by shouting, due to the noise around us. Most of the passengers were American GIs, headed home to the United States. Almost all of the faces showed joyful excitement, but there were also tears of parting from those who stayed behind. Then we heard the orders to start sailing, the ropes were winched aboard, and the ship, slowly pulled by two tugboats, started on its course. There was a flurry of waving both from those aboard and from those standing on the pier as the ship moved towards the open sea. My sister Inge was on her way to New York City. An uncle of ours, who had fled Germany before the Nazis took over, now lived in New York City and had sponsored Inge, enabling her to emigrate to the United States. It was ten long years before Inge and I met again in Germany.

Our entire family was determined to leave this Germany where we had experienced so much persecution and misery. Two years after my sister emigrated, my parents went to New Zealand to stay with relatives of my mother. During this journey, while briefly in Paris, my mother contracted a very severe case of flu, which could not be cured. The seven-week-long voyage from Marseilles was made bearable only by heavy doses of medicine and she never recovered from the kidney ailment that resulted from this heavy medication. I also planned to emigrate to New Zealand as soon as my parents had established themselves there and were able to sponsor us. I had become a proud father when my wife Hannelore gave birth to a girl. Hannelore rejected my plans to emigrate; she wanted to stay in Germany.

I had resigned my position at the Brose Company, since the former owners had taken over again. The "deNazification" process of the victorious Allies had hit a snag in the course of political changes. The western Allies needed the Germans, including the Nazis, in their cold war against Russia and her satellite nations in eastern Europe. The past cruelties of the Nazis were ignored, and they appeared again in their old positions everywhere. The German Justice Department, which had been a willing tool of Hitler, immediately recognized this change, and it was nearly an honor again to have been a Nazi.

Then I received the news from my father that the building in Auckland, New Zealand, that housed the immigration department, where my application rested, had been burned down. Was this a hint of fate? My sister had meanwhile pursued my application for immigration into the United States, and finally the time had come. I received my permit. But fate was against me again. The Korean War broke out, and I could count on being drafted and shipped out to Korea shortly after my arrival in the United States. Had I survived the terrible era of the Nazi dictatorship, and the most destructive of all wars without a scratch, just so I could fight in Korea for some very questionable goals of political power? No! Then I would rather remain in Germany, which was now slowly recovering from the scars of war.

In order to pass the time until my visa was granted, I had opened a photography studio, and worked for a regional newspaper as a writer of advertising copy. On the side I wrote reports for a daily newspaper in Coburg, and also modelled figurines for the Goebel company. Thus I was able to earn enough for our basic needs. Unfortunately, I received very little support from my wife. She came from a professional family, and had learned no trade or profession other than housekeeping. When we were married, I had a good position, a big car and a certain influence in Coburg, but those times were over now.

Since my plans for emigration were somewhere down a foggy road, I had to build a secure foundation for now. Everything I had done up to now did not satisfy me, and did not bring me any success. One day I was sitting again in the executive office of the Goebel company, and sold several clay models to Franz Goebel. He remarked worriedly that his sculptors Arthur Moeller and Reinhold Unger were getting on in age, and that there was no talented replacement in sight. Was this perhaps the chance of a lifetime? I proposed to Mr. Goebel that he give me a shot at it. He didn't want to hear about it. "We know each other too well for you to be in my employment, and besides, you know very little about porcelain manufacturing. All the models you create have to be reworked by my master modelers. And it will be no fun to work with the two old modelers!"

But I didn't give up that easily, and asked him to give me a chance to study the various phases of production. At the same time, I would keep sculpting figurines for him, and eventually would even make the molds. "And how do you want to provide for your family?" he asked me. But finally we agreed that I should give it a try. At first I would receive the wages of a skilled worker. That was not very much, but by supplementing my income with modeling, photography and writing newspaper articles, I could get by. In parting, Franz Goebel said to me: "You will see that you cannot make a go of it. My workers are capable people, but they have rough manners. You are not used to that, and they won't make life easy for you. But I'll keep an eye on you." With that, we shook hands on my new position as co-worker, and the first step into a promising future had been taken.

A Tough Beginning
Spring 1952

The plaster of Paris made a whistling noise as I drew the steel knife across it in order to smooth out the last rough spots. Again I scrutinized the master mold very carefully. I had created the mold from all the parts of the Hummel figurine #152B, "Umbrella Girl." The umbrella itself made the largest mold, the two halves of which were lying in front of me on my perfectly leveled work desk. I had a problem with the casting hole, which I had carved into both halves with my putty knife. In order to cut the funnel accurately in the casting department, a small strip had to remain at the seam of the lower half of the mold. Accidentally, by exerting too much pressure on the knife, I had cut away this strip in one place. I filled the space again with fresh plaster of Paris, and smoothed it over so that it would fit the upper half of the mold. At this moment, master mold maker Schmidt stepped behind me, raised the mold, and critically eyed the once-again fitting form and remarked: "Well, this time you lucked out! You have to be very careful that you do not pare too much off."

Master Schmidt was a very experienced specialist, and a very good teacher. He knew all the problems that could arise during the manufacture of molds and the working with plaster of Paris—and there were many of them. When others were dumbfounded about a problem, he would give his advice and solution with a smug smile. I had now been in the department of plaster of Paris molds for more than a half year, had learned a lot, and had even made suggestions for improvements. But there was still so much to learn, and I had to acquire

more practical knowledge in this extremely complex area. The manufacturing of plaster of Paris molds is actually the tool and die shop of
a porcelain factory. It can happen that a beautiful sculpted clay model
can be completely ruined by sloppy work in the creation of the mother
mold. On the other hand, even the best mold maker will have a lot
of problems with a model created by an unqualified person. Preci-
sion in work, and a high degree of experience, are the necessary requirements for successful production. Each model has its own problem areas. The process starts with the cutting up of the figurine into
the individual mold parts. Very often, a model or parts of a model
have to be changed by the sculptor, especially when one is trying to
keep the price of the finished piece down. From what material is the
figurine to be made? And are there, especially with porcelain, supports necessary during the firing stage? Also, the method of decorating a figurine plays an important part in this consideration. All these
problems and many more have to be discussed with the various spe-
cialists to assure that everything will run smooth during the production process. Still, one encounters numerous problems that have to
be solved in regularly scheduled discussions. As long as porcelain figurines are produced, problems will come up and have to be solved.

Quitting time was approaching in the plaster of Paris department.
Everybody had finished his or her work with the molds. Here and
there somebody was cleaning up, or etching model numbers into the
mold, or marking the mother molds with red paint to ensure that
everybody would use extreme care with those. Then the knives, drawing knives, scrapers and the many special tools were cleaned and
wiped with an oil rag in order to prevent rusting. I had constructed a
cone-shaped drill in order to facilitate the cutting of the funnel holes
into the finished molds, and my prior technical knowledge had helped
me in this undertaking. Then the bell rang, and everybody jumped
up in order to get home as soon as possible. At home, most had to
tend to a garden or to a field, or to assist a neighbor with the construction of his house. Even more work awaited the women: getting the
children from kindergarten, shopping, dinner preparations and other
household tasks.

In a short while only the department head, who was caught up
in paperwork, and I remained. So I got started on my evening work.
From the wet box I took the model of a madonna and set it on the
turntable in front of me. The face did not yet have the right expres-

sion, one I had admired in the madonnas sculpted by Reinhold Unger. I intended to sell this model to the Goebel company and thus bolster my income. The practical experience of mold making was already affecting my work in modeling. When I began the sketch of a model, I was already considering the later mold-making process, using my experiences as a guideline. When my model was accepted by Franz Goebel, I created the master mold myself.

Franz Goebel personally inspected my clay models, and I always admired his keen eye for essential details. He also possessed an uncanny sense for the marketability of a figurine, or a series of figurines. He was very rarely wrong in his impulse. He was the born "patriarch," and did not tolerate objections. If someone criticized him, he could become very gruff. Franz Goebel was of very short stature, but had a very big heart. If someone was in dire need, he provided help without giving it much thought. I got along with him very well, probably because I am also short. "I have a lot of big plans with you," he said, "but first you have to learn a lot." I took his advice to heart, and tried to acquire as much knowledge as possible about the manufacturing of porcelain, and to let this knowledge influence me in my sculpting. Only this way was it possible to create something outstanding in this very interesting and manifold field.

This time of ambitious studying and striving was broken by shattering news from New Zealand: my mother had passed away. It took me a long time to recover from this blow. I had always gotten along very well with my mother.

In the same year, my second daughter was born. Our marriage was in trouble, and we were not planning another child. But it happened, and we called her Victoria.

The Decision
May 1954

I was sitting in the chief executive's office with butterflies in my stomach. Across from me sat Franz Goebel, on whose desk I had placed the first synthetic resin working model—the result of experiments in the kitchen of my home. Up to now, the working models (or the block and case, as they were also called) which were used in the manufacture of molds had been made out of plaster of Paris throughout the porcelain industry. These molds were soaked in linseed oil, and dried in an oven, in order to make them leak-proof and to harden the surfaces. One could only cast between thirty to fifty working molds from these mother molds, because the finer details wear away in the process and are eventually erased.

Due to increased production over the past few years, more and more working molds were required. All parts of a figurine had to be cast in plaster of Paris, fitted to the completed figurine, and then master molds had to be cast for the individual parts, in order to replenish the working molds. The proportions of an individual figurine changed through the expansion of the plaster of Paris, the pinching of the seams and the fitting of the single pieces into the figurine. The necks grew longer, the arms and legs were not round anymore, and the figurines themselves grew larger. The quality of the Hummel figurines, which were produced in ever-increasing numbers, became rapidly poorer, and it was only a matter of time until a negative reaction from the market would

48

make itself felt. Karl Litzow, who had recently became our technical director (after having been the head of a ceramic specialty school), recognized these problems and acted.

He went through the entire factory and collected all the older figurines, then displayed them in special showcases according to the specific numbers (sizes). Thus it was very easy for him to discern by comparison the deviations in proportions and sizes between the older figurines and those being produced now. The deviation was most evident with figurine #129, "Bandleader," where the latest figurine, produced in 1951, is more than one inch taller than the oldest model dating from 1939. Karl Litzow had tried in vain to persuade the old modelers, Mr. Moeller and Mr. Unger, to create new clay models for these figurines to bring them down to the same size and proportion of the old figurines.

In the past years I had come to know the many problems in the manufacturing of porcelain, and especially in the production of working molds, which seemed very complicated, and for which plaster of Paris had been used exclusively. Thus grew my idea to produce the working molds out of a harder material, which could also be cold-cast, instead of plaster of Paris.

At the Hanover Trade Fair I discovered the first synthetic resin, which was, like plaster of Paris, pourable, and which became, through the cold-casting process, a material as hard as iron, due to a hardener that was mixed into it and contained the necessary acids. I made my experiments with this new material, and developed, through a very special procedure, a working model that was immune to distortions, and from which I had cast a well-fitting working form.

Franz Goebel looked very intently at that model and at the plaster of Paris mold, as well as at the porcelain head I had cast from the new mold. Then he reached for the telephone and asked Mr. Litzow and the head of our laboratory, Mrs. Lehmann, to come to his office. They had hardly entered his office when Franz Goebel said, in his gruff voice: "I have built a very expensive laboratory for you here, and Skrobek developed this model out of synthetic resin in the kitchen of his home!"

An embarrassing silence followed. I had the feeling that my days at Goebel were numbered, because these two would never forgive me. Their defense—that they also had done experiments in that direction but never concluded them on account of other more pressing projects—was swept aside by Franz Goebel with the remark: "But you did not accomplish anything!" Happily, I was quite wrong. This memorable discussion was the beginning of a close and fruitful collaboration between Karl Litzow and myself. He apparently recognized that I had the technical and artistic ability to restore the Hummel figurines to a high standard of quality.

The Bird–Watcher

April 1955

In my hand I held an old sample of a Hummel figurine out of the master mold. I turned it in all directions, and inspected it very carefully. Even then the Merry Wanderer with his big satchel was already the symbol of the M.I. Hummel collection; he seemed to stroll into the world with childlike curiosity, full of expectations. Then I compared the old sample with a model from a recent production: what a difference! The childlike proportions had changed; the neck was too long and the hands were too crude. The child's face with its rounded cheeks had turned into a flat profile. Secretly, Karl Litzow had ordered me to re-mold some of the older Hummel figurines from his storeroom in clay, singling out those that really needed re-molding. The old figurines he had collected became the foundation for the Hummel archives. Before he had started collecting these, old models were simply thrown away, or even broken, once they looked their age. This archive became an invaluable asset in later years, as we compared its stock against new production pieces.

Litzow had also immediately recognized the importance of the synthetic-resin working models I had developed for maintaining a consistent quality in the production of the M.I. Hummel figurines. He saw to it that the Goebel company look over my invention, for which I had already applied for a patent.

With great energy and enthusiasm I took over my new responsibilities, often working late into the night. This way I could also avoid someone discovering my secret work with the Hummel figurines. I hid my models way in back of the "wet" cabinet and put my other figurines in front of them. I not only studied old samples, but also wandered through the various offices where many of Sister Hummel's original paintings hung on the walls. I also collected all the Hummel postcards and books, like *Die Hummel,* I could find. In this way I tried to gather as much knowledge as possible about the life and art of Sister Hummel. But all this had to be done in secret, without anybody noticing.

Finally the day came when Karl Litzow and I presented Franz Goebel with the newly remodeled Hummel figurines for his approval. At first he didn't want to have anything to do with the project. "What will Moeller and Unger say when they find out that we are creating new models of Hummel figurines behind their backs?" was his comment. Only after Litzow pointed out that the two had rejected the remodeling did Goebel give the new models a second look. After a long silence, he said, "We have to present these to the convent for their approval," and then dismissed us.

Litzow now gave me the order to model a new Hummel figurine, which had not been in production so far. He handed me a photograph from which I was to copy the new figurine. It was a charcoal sketch of a little boy feeding birds in the winter. I went to work on it immediately, and soon the finished model was standing in front of me. We gave it the mold number 233, and entered it into the model log book under my name. This figurine was also praised by Reinhold Unger, who assisted me in the years to come with his great experience, and from whom I learned a great deal. Arthur Moeller, however, had only very reluctantly agreed to the premise that other sculptors were to work on Hummel figurines from now on. My colleague at that time, Menzenbach, was also ordered to start modeling Hummel figurines. Later on other sculptors were employed as well. They, however, created very few figurines. At the request of the convent, I had to redo most of their models.

One day Franz Goebel called me into his office. "Sit down," he said in his usual way, because he did not like it if someone stood in front of him. He told me, "we will make a new beginning," and handed me a big black ledger. "This will be the new log of Hummel models, and I entrust you to keep it up. You will start with number 300. The open number below that shall be reserved for special issues."

At the age of two, I took a ride on a sled with my mother. This 1924
photo is strikingly similar to the M.I. Hummel figurine entitled
"Ride into Christmas."

My mother created this painting in 1914.

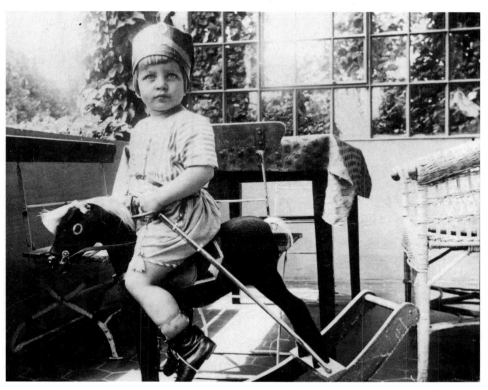

I was a proud two-year-old rocking-horse rider.

This formal 1939 portrait captured me as a 17-year-old.

My parents celebrated their silver wedding anniversary in September 1944. Two months later, my father was sent to a labor camp.

This 1950 photo is of my first wife, Hannelore.

My two-and-a-half-year-old
daughter, Suzanne, posed
as a little wash girl in 1949.

I snapped my second
daughter, Victoria, in this
typically two-year-old
posture in 1955.

In my early years at Goebel, I once worked with the American artist Huldah Jeffe. This 1959 photo shows me sculpting, with Huldah Jeffe next to me. To our left are: Utz Stocke, standing, Mr. Wick from Crestwick and, on the other side of Huldah Jeffe, Franz Goebel. (Photo courtesy of Goebel)

Franz Goebel and I often visited the Convent of Siessen to discuss forthcoming figurines. In 1964 the meeting group included, from left: Mother Superior Maria Angela, Franz Goebel, Sister Berta, Father Superior Gresser and myself.

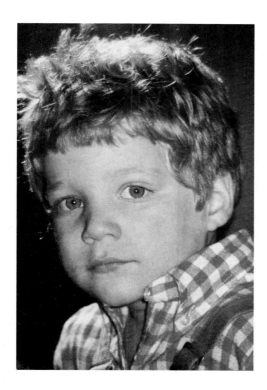

My second wife, Sieglinde, and I have two sons, Martin, at left, who was born in 1969, and Stephan, born in 1972. At the time of these photos, Martin was four years old and Stephan was two years old.

I greatly enjoyed the chance to make a close study of a falcon in preparation for a new sculpture in 1968. (Photo courtesy of Goebel)

In 1978 Joan Ostroff of Goebel and I judged the M.I. Hummel Look-Alike Contest during the M.I. Hummel Festival in Eaton, Ohio.

In 1981 I was able to visit with my cousin Sonja, whom I had not seen in many years, in Des Moines, Iowa, where she lived.

In 1979 I was able to indulge in one of my favorite pastimes, scuba diving, in the Virgin Islands.

On a 1979 visit to the Convent of Siessen, I studied some of the pieces in the sample collection. With me are, from left to right: Sister Domenica, Sister Berta, Mother Superior Radegundis, and Dieter Schneider of Goebel.

Several representatives from Goebel met with the sisters at the Convent of Siessen on this day in March 1985. From left we are: Sister Radegundis, Sister Witgard, and representing Goebel, Dieter Schneider, Dieter Eckstein, myself and Herbert Hennig.

In 1984 I had the privilege of meeting with President Carstens of the
Federal Republic of Germany in Ashaffenburg. President Carsstens is
on the far right in this photo; I am in the left foreground.
(Photo courtesy of Borowski)

I posed with this 1987 tour group in front of the restaurant Rosenan just before a candlelight dinner. (Photo courtesy of Goebel)

Sieglinde and I enjoyed the Franconian Evening celebrated in Coburg with the Goebel Collector's Club tour in 1987.

Then he summoned Litzow and marketing director Vier and told them, "I want to establish a development department under his direction" (pointing at me), "completely closed off from everything else. This is the place where the Hummel figurines will be developed, from the modeling stage to the final painting, and no one shall have access to this department except those employed there." As the Hummel figurines grew more and more popular, more and more copies and imitations were appearing, mostly from Japan but also from other countries. There were long and costly legal proceedings to secure the copyrights. Franz Goebel explained that by closing off the development department he wanted to protect the Hummel figurines from being copied before they came on the market.

Then he jumped to another topic. "We have to establish more personal contact with the convent," he said. "As soon as a larger number of clay models and samples is finished, my brother-in-law Eux, together with Skrobek and Unger, shall drive out to Siessen and discuss the individual figurines with the appropriate staff at the convent." Dr. Eugen Stocke had gotten up from his desk and walked over to where we were assembled. He agreed wholeheartedly to Franz's idea, and planned to contact the convent and set a date when all could meet.

The Eux Pool

June 1955

Neptune had arisen from the waters, and his imposing hulk stood before a wildly applauding crowd. Water was dripping from his long green hair and from the wreaths of plants wrapped around his mighty belly. He pounded his trident three times on the tiled floor, and announced in a sonorous voice: "I christen thee The Eux Pool. May you give enjoyment and refreshment to all those who submerge in your waters." To the accompaniment of applause from the surrounding crowd, he departed to return to a civilian life. Then we unveiled the memorial plaque, and emptied our glasses.

The christening was followed by a number of sporting events, including a lovely water ballet. All the performers were employees of the company, and participated with great enthusiasm. After the inauguration of the pool that bore Dr. Stocke's name, his 60th birthday celebration could begin. We had worked late into the night before, taking the memorial plaque out of the form and smoothing it. We had poured the plaster of Paris mold for the plaque only the day before. As usual, the idea for it had come up at the very last moment. The architect for the pool project came to me three days before the unveiling, and begged me to take this project into my own hands. He told me: "I know there is not much time, but we have to erect a memorial plaque. You can probably think of something very special." Then he gave me a pleading look. I had no choice but to take the project over. Then I had the idea of fashioning the stone in the shape of the pool. I had made the medallion that was given to all the participants in this shape. I also intended to etch the water nymph from the medallion into the stone. So we went to work.

A young modeler carved the basic shape out of a plaster-of-Paris slab. Another shaped the individual letters for the inscription, and I designed the relief form of the nymph in the correct proportion. This way, we were all finished at approximately the same time, and could transfer the various elements onto the model plate. We also carved a pedestal with the appropriate devices for mounting the plaque out of plaster of Paris, and then cast molds from these parts. Three large containers of plaster of Paris were barely enough for fashioning this huge form. It was already late in the evening when we were able to take the individual pieces out of their forms. Then all the parts from the form were smoothed over, and set next to the porcelain kiln for drying. It was midnight when I got home.

Early the following morning, we began to fill in the letters and the water nymph with white cement. After thoroughly cleaning the needed area, we spread artificial sandstone on it. Three of us tamped this material into the form, watching carefully that there were no air bubbles. Since time was of the essence, the company mason had mixed a cement mixture that would harden very fast—we had only until that evening to let everything set. Everything went according to plan, and just before the ceremony was to start we were able to erect the commemorative stone.

All this hard and tedious work was forgotten once the festivities began, and all the participants were caught up in a merry mood. Everyone had received coupons to redeem for bratwurst, beer, wine, cola and chocolates. Everything was plentiful, and nobody could be hungry or thirsty. A band played dance music, and soon the festive mood reached its pinnacle. I, too, wanted to dance, but for a short person it is not an easy task to find a suitable partner. Then I discovered Daniela, who worked in the laboratory and with whom I had become friendly. We matched in size, and soon we were spinning across the dance floor to the tune of a Viennese waltz. Franz Goebel spotted us, and waved us over to his table, where he presented us with glasses of champagne, and offered a toast: "I really liked your memorial stone. You did an excellent job, and on Monday morning I want to see you in my office." He gave me a friendly jab. "And you found a very pretty partner," he concluded, and turned to his other guests.

Thus we celebrated as one big family—the often-mentioned Goebel Family—until the wee hours of the morning. At Daniela's apartment, which was close to the factory, I had a cup of coffee, then went to the Oeslau train station and took the first train to Coburg. So ended one of many company festivals at Goebel in which I participated. In the following days there was, of course, a lot of gossip, and I was not spared, since Daniela was a very pretty girl.

At the Siessen Convent

July 1955

Dr. Stocke was driving at a pretty good clip—about 100 miles per hour—on the Itzengrund road just outside of Coburg, which was laced with sharp turns. He evidently enjoyed it when the tires squealed, and grinned at Director Litzow who was sitting next to him. They were talking about the scheduled visit to the Siessen convent, and hoped that most of the new Hummel figurines, securely stashed in the trunk of the car, would be approved by the Convent. Reinhold Unger was sitting next to me in the back, and at each turn he gripped the handle above the door, growing paler by the minute. He whispered to me, "I am already an old man, and have my life behind me, in case we do not survive this trip. But you are far too young to die now." I smiled at him reassuringly. "Dr. Stocke is an accomplished driver," I said. "Nothing will happen to us today." This speedy traveling was a new experience for Reinhold Unger, and one that scared him; he had always gone by train. But after a while, he got used to the tempo. He looked out the window at the beautiful landscape passing by and slowly seemed to enjoy traveling in the car. Besides, everything went well during this five-hour trip through southern Germany. At that time, many of today's autobahns and bypasses had not yet been constructed, and we had to travel through many towns and small villages during this memorable trip, my first visit to the Siessen Convent in the summer of 1955.

We had room reservations at the traditional Kleber Post hotel in Saulgau, and checked in upon our arrival. Sister M.I. Hummel's parents had always stayed here when they visited their daughter, and had established a close relationship with the owners. Since we had some time to kill before dinner, we took a stroll through Saulgau, a very clean little Swabian city. During the excellent meal, we again discussed the next day's plans. Dr. Stocke ordered a very good wine, and we all drank a toast to the successful conclusion of our presentation.

The following morning, after an enjoyable breakfast, we set out for the Convent, which soon loomed in front of us on top of a hill. It was a drive of only a few miles. Traveling down a country lane lined with tall trees, we soon arrived at the Convent's courtyard and stood at the gate, loaded down with our packages. The gatekeeper, a nun, opened the gate and greeted us: "You must be the gentlemen from the Goebel Company! We are already expecting you." She escorted us to the visitors' room, where Reinhold Unger and I immediately began to carefully unpack the new Hummel figurines. We placed them on the conference table in the order of their production numbers. We heard voices in the hall outside, and then two elderly nuns stepped into the room, Sister Laura and Sister Waltrude. Dr. Stocke introduced us and relayed greetings from the Goebel and Stocke families, in particular a greeting from his brother-in-law, Franz Goebel. Sister Laura had attended the Munich Art School with Sister Maria Innocentia, and had instilled in her the desire to join the Siessen Convent. Sister Laura was an accomplished artist in her own right, had been Sister Maria Innocentia's closest associate, and had made many excellent copies from Sister Maria Innocentia's original art work. Sister Waltrude, an art teacher, had been entrusted with the Convent's administrative duties.

Sister Laura looked at all the figurines we had displayed on the table and said, "Now, let us have a look at the new figurines you want to show us for our approval." She took the first piece in her hand, put it on the little turntable in the middle of the table and turned it slowly around so that she could see it from all directions. After a while, she nodded in agreement: "This figurine has turned out well; only the green on the dress could be a little lighter." And so, she took one figurine after the other, inspecting the positions, the proportions, the expressions and the coloring compared to the original drawing by Sister Hummel. I had prepared notes in which I jotted down any objection or unfavorable critique. Then came the first shock: The initial two figurines that we presented, two trees with angels modeled by A. Moeller, were rejected by Sister Laura. She did not like the arrangement of the figurines, since it did not comply with the more ornately done drawing. "I could accept these figurines by themselves, but not in a combination with these trees," she said. No other objections were raised during the rest of the figurines' inspection. On some, Sister Laura requested some changes, particularly in the painting. During a break in an adjoining room, I talked to her at length about Sister Maria Innocentia. She answered all my questions patiently, sensing how important this information would be for my future projects. I found out many details about Maria Innocentia that had never been mentioned in the books about her. Her personality appeared to me in a new light: She was a very happy woman, with a keen sense of beauty, deeply religious without an ostentatious display of her faith. Very often, her humorous, sometimes even impish nature shone through. Her charming (but also critical) humor, combined with a great sense of fantasy, and her ingenuity, coupled with a unique artistic talent, enabled her to create a multitude of children's portraits in many situations. Even in the roughest of times at the convent, during the last years of World War II, Maria Innocentia was able to spread some joy among the other sisters to cheer them up. At that time, she drew most of her children with smiles on their faces. This discussion with Sister Laura, with whom I met only once more the following year, was of the greatest importance to me in the creation of Hummel figurines.

When all the new figurines had been discussed, we packed up the lot again. Those models that had been accepted were left at the Convent as reference samples. Entirely satisfied with our success, we started our journey home, accompanied by the sisters' many good wishes.

"Ring Around the Rosie"
Summer 1957

"I would turn the head of the foremost girl a little more to the front, so that it is looking even more towards the viewer," advised Reinhold Unger when I showed him the clay model of the four dancing girls. His critique was very valuable to me because he had had decades of experience in modeling, and his judgment was foolproof. Over time, we had developed a very collegial relationship. Reinhold Unger was a very straightforward man who spoke his mind, and I had received many valuable tips from him. The lovely faces of his children and madonnas inspired me in my own work.

I spun the turntable a little so that the girls really seemed to dance. "The motion is very well done. They really look alive; however, the skirt of the girl on the left could use a little more 'flight'," Unger said, as he returned to his work area. I took some clay, applied it to the pleat of the skirt, smoothed it with my finger, and in that way enlarged the outer fold of the skirt in the direction of the rotation. It looked a lot better and livelier. Then I began the tedious perfecting of the details; the faces, the hair and braids, and all the other little things had to be carefully modeled in a figurine group of this size. In order to achieve the natural look of the dancing girls holding hands, I had done quite a few anatomic studies using live models. That proved to be immensely helpful for this project. My teacher at the Reimann Institute had a saying: "The observation of living nature cannot be replaced by anything." I always heeded this advice, to my advantage.

Finally, after many weeks of work, the model of the four danc-ing girls was finished, even though it seemed as if the work was never done on such a special and elaborate figure. There is always a spot here and there that could be improved; nothing is so perfect that it could not be done even better. But time was of the essence, and even-tually I put down my tools and finished the model. It can easily hap-pen that after a day or two, you look at the model and find places for improvement here and there—and the cycle begins anew. However, during the process of retouching the master model, there is always an opportunity to make small alterations. We would be making an-other presentation at the convent very soon so I carefully scanned the model. Then I wrapped it in waterproof foil and carefully packed it in a container lined with styrofoam so it would survive the long jour-ney without being damaged.

The reaction of the Convent to the model of the four dancing girls was just great. "This is really a masterpiece," exclaimed Sister Maria Angela, who, as Mother Superior, had been attending the pre-sentations for some time. Sister Berta, legal heir to Sister Maria Inno-centia's estate, was very impressed with my work. "A well-done figu-rine—the girls really seem to dance. Maria Innocentia would have been very proud of this model," she said. Sister Berta and I not only had something in common—our short stature—but we also got along very well in other respects, exchanging our experiences in fixing pho-tographic problems. We almost became friends in the course of our encounters over the decades.

The painting arrangement of the dancing girls that we presented at our next visit to the Convent was approved by the sisters. During the ensuing discussion, it was decided to release this special piece for the 25th anniversary of the M.I. Hummel figurines. Even today, after more than 30 years, this figurine is one of the most popular in the Hummel collection.

Artists from the United States
Summer 1958

With bold strokes of her experienced, talented hands, Charlot Byj drew a madonna in front of a freestanding dovecote. This was the third time she had drawn it after we had discussed the motif at length. Her first sketches could have been transferred into a three-dimensional piece without great trouble, but now she had created a picture that I could model without any drastic changes.

Even though Charlot Byj knew exactly what she wanted, she never hesitated to compromise when it was necessary. We had been working together for more than two weeks now, ever since she had arrived from the States, and quite a few new clay models were sitting on the shelves of the "wetting" cabinet. Most of these were children, extensions of her "red-head" series. But now she had drawn several madonnas in an unconventional way, all of which portrayed a very close mother and child relationship. The Madonna of the Doves would no doubt be the most complicated piece in this series; yet, it was later the most successful one. In contrast to the children with their comical expressions, these madonnas were done in a rather naturalistic style and so perhaps attracted more collectors. Over the years, I worked with Charlot Byj quite often, in the Goebel studios, as well as in the United States. We created an atmosphere of artistic trust and confidence between us, which bore fruit in the results of our mutual cooperation. Charlot Byj lived a very secluded life in New York, and was already very ill during my later visits, when we discussed the clay models that I had brought. She did not show up for our last scheduled meeting; she had passed away the day before. Her Madonna of the Doves, which had always been her favorite motif, is a figurine that is still bought and appreciated by collectors around the world.

Huldah Jeffe, a member of New York City society, painted in the style of the French Impressionists. She had been invited by Franz Goebel to create figurines based on her art, with the help of our staff. I was very skeptical about this project from the beginning, since the Impressionistic style, with its faded outlines, can hardly be expressed in the third dimension. I mentioned this to Franz Goebel but he thought we should give it a try. So, in an atmosphere of cooperation, we created a number of figurines and gift items. A number of other sculptors besides me participated in this project. We tried in vain to imbue some of the charm of the Huldah paintings into the figurines— alas, we were unsuccessful. In this case, the fundamental difference between a two-dimensional picture and a three-dimensional figurine became all too evident. Only artistic expressions with very clear outlines can be successfully transformed into figurines, as is clear in the production of the M.I. Hummel pieces.

The situation with Janet Robson, another artist from the United States, was quite different. (Unfortunately, this very talented woman also has passed away.) Some of the religious figurines based on her art work were created decades ago and are still in the Goebel "standard" collection. Besides her work in the greeting card industry, she also drew designs for church windows, which require a very high level of artistic ability.

I really enjoyed working with Janet. She drew charming religious motifs in her own quiet way. She left us a generous amount of leeway in transforming her drawings into figurines so that we could show off our own artistic talents. In this way, we all contributed to the best of our abilities, and the result was a successful line.

Working with these different artists from the United States was very interesting; they all had their own creative personalities. Through these people, I was able to form an opinion about the American artistic interests, which are so different from those of Europeans and which are expressed in the artistic products that they collect. This can be traced to the differences in historical development.

Modern Art

August 1958

There it stood in front of me, larger than a man, and made of shiny aluminum. The entwined surfaces only remotely hinted at human beings, yet seemed to flow with motion. I had stepped back a few paces after I had polished the last rough surfaces. While looking at this sculpture, I began to doubt whether I was on the right track after all with this metal creation. I had spent my entire two-week vacation here in the factory's machine shop; I had sawed, cut, welded, riveted and glued. From early morning until late into the night, I had worked while my colleagues were enjoying their time off. I heard some snide, sarcastic remarks about this piece from some employees in the machine shop, but most of the workers praised my work and offered valuable advice.

It had all started with the planning of a large exhibition by our artists' guild, of which I was a very active member. We had staged some shows in years past that had received very good reviews. This time, though, the exhibition was supposed to be a very extravagant one, and during our discussions, the possibility of showing abstract art came up. This idea hit home with me; I thought about it constantly and I started not only to visualize a concept but began to work on it. I made sketches and drafts, and was soon determined to try my hand at a metal sculpture, using my experiences in metalworking that I had acquired during the war. The sculpture would not be small and dainty, but of an impressive size, thus satisfying my own aspirations. One of my sketches seemed to be quite suitable: two dancing figures, which, even though rendered as abstracts, were still recognizable as humans.

I could see this creation in my imagination, but I was a long way from making it a reality. It was impossible to work on such a large project at home, and my spare time was very limited; I even had to work on Saturdays at the factory. Then, it occurred to me that I could do it on my vacation and use all the equipment in the machine shop. Franz Goebel, who was always open to special activities, allowed me to do this. Our technical office was instrumental in helping me to find the necessary aluminum profiles and sheets that I needed for the project. The machine-shop supervisor gave me a crash course in the difficult art of welding aluminum. Then I was ready to begin.

First I outlined the shapes of the over-sized figures on cardboard sheets and cut them out. I transferred these patterns onto the aluminum sheets and with metal shears, cut them out in duplicate—a more than tedious process. Soon I had blisters on hands that were unused to this kind of work. But I did not give up! I simply wore soft gloves over my bandaged hands. Then I had to bend the side profiles, saw them, and weld them together in many places. I then anchored the entire structure to a prepared base and glued the preshaped sheets onto the profiles with a special adhesive. It all sounds very simple, but there were many problems in handling the metal. I often wished that I had had four hands. My experience in metalworking was invaluable; without it, I never would have accomplished this piece. The two weeks, with their hard toil, had ended, and my concept began to take shape. Despite all of my initial doubts as to the artistic value of my project, I was proud of it, and I looked forward to the opening of the exhibition. Even Franz Goebel came to see it and spoke favorably of it.

There was still a lot to do until the exhibition opened in the fall, and I had to sacrifice a great deal of my spare time. Attendance was very good at the opening and throughout the show, the local papers gave it good coverage, reporting about the art works in detail; my Ice-Dance, as I had named my sculpture, received lavish praise. The mayor of Coburg was so impressed by my creation that he considered giving it a permanent place in front of the municipal auditorium (or Kongresshaus, as it is known). Nothing came of that idea because the city architect had chosen another statue. But he died before he could carry out his plan and, to this day, there is no piece of art gracing the Kongresshaus. After this excursion into the world of abstract art, I again devoted my talents to the naturalistic form, and have stayed with that since then.

Mingling with the Stars
Winter 1958

"Camera on. Sound on." The man with the "take sign" stepped forward, the director hollered "Action" and the scene was played for the sixth time. This continued until both the director and the camera man were satisfied. For the past three days, I had been at the movie studios in Berlin. The director's assistant had assigned me a seat behind the props, out of camera range. Of course, this arrangement changed with each new setting, and I had to change seats quite frequently. There I was, sitting on a stool, surrounded by heavy cables, props, pieces of odd wood and whatever else you might find lying around a sound stage. Through an opening in the props, I could study my model who was standing a few yards away: Bibi Jones, a well-known singer and actress in Germany during the 1950s. I was sculpting her head in a size of only two inches; I held the head on a stick in my left hand while I worked on it with my right hand. These were really very unusual circumstances for modeling a portrait, but there were no other options. Like most successful actresses, Bibi Jones had very little free time. I was only able to study her thoroughly and compare her to my clay piece during the short recesses between shots. Bibi Jones was a very attractive woman, not arrogant at all, and we got along well. We had interesting discussions about our artistic activities, which were, of course, in completely different fields. While I stressed her acting abilities and her popularity with the public, she admired her likeness, which was taking shape in my hands. It was her opinion that people would admire my creations for generations to come, while her movies

66

and recordings would gather dust in some archives. The time just seemed to fly, and when the shooting of the movie ended for the day, I was pretty much finished with my sculpture. Before I said goodbye to Bibi, I took a series of snapshots of her, and a very busy, interesting day came to a close.

Franz Goebel had given me the assignment of creating movie star "dolls." These dolls were supposed to be lifelike, but no matter how many photographs of an object I looked at, I knew that this was not the way to do it. I could only achieve this goal by studying the live model. So I flew to Berlin with my modeling clay and sculpting tools. People in the know had advised me not to drive to Berlin through East Germany. Since I was a specialist in optical instruments, it could very well be that my name was on a Russian "wanted" list, and I was not the least interested in being dragged off to the USSR.

After a ten-year interval, this was my first visit to the city where I had spent my adolescent years. Not all of the heavy wartime damage to the buildings had been repaired. I encountered ruins almost everywhere: bombed-out shells and vacant lots filled with rubble, especially in the eastern part of the city. The secretary of the Film Union, which was a socialist institution of all persons associated with movie making, took care of me during my stay there. He also took me for a ride through the Soviet sector of Berlin. When I started to photograph the crumbling balconies of the recently completed "show" buildings on Stalin Boulevard, my driver yanked me back inside the car. The dreaded Volkspolizei (People's Police) would not understand my nosiness, he said.

I had to get up very early the next morning since I had to be in Caterina Valente's dressing room at 7 am, where I could work on my sculpture of her during her two-hour make-up and hairstyling session. When I arrived, she was already there and, after a brief introduction, I started my work, which I had already roughly shaped in clay, using photographs of her. However, when I wanted to take additional pictures of her, she consented only after I solemnly promised that none of these photographs would ever be published. I was to use them solely for my portrait model. During the next two hours, I witnessed the make-up artist transform Caterina, who was getting on in years, into a radiant beauty; that is the way I modeled her. I then understood why she did not wish to have photographs showing her without make-up or the proper hairdo published—it wouldn't have helped her image as the "eternally young" Caterina Valente!

Movie personnel constantly came into the dressing room to discuss questions they had about the film. Caterina treated each one with special courtesy, some with an air of servility, even. She could be a little bit difficult, but to me she was a human being like anyone else, despite her fame. I always tried to approach people with the same friendliness, whether they were famous or unknown, rich or poor. By doing this, we got along beautifully from the very beginning; I was even under the impression that she was particularly courteous to me. It's not easy being a famous star, and some of them display an air of defensiveness or aloofness that is not simple to pierce.

"All done," said the make-up artist. Caterina looked at the clock, got up from her chair and said goodbye to me. Her parting words were "See you tomorrow morning!" Glancing at the small clay head that I had modeled, she said, "That is already a very good likeness." And she went out the door. "Caterina is always on time," the make-up artist told me, and just then, my chauffeur showed up.

In another studio, I was introduced to "Aze" Brauner, the movie company's director. He wished me luck in my work and escorted me to my next assignment. I asked him about film director Paul Verhoeven, with whom I had been well acquainted for many years. He replied that Verhoeven was shooting movies in Munich, as was Heinz Ruehmann, who was a famous comic movie star.

When we arrived at the studio, everyone was on break, so I was introduced to my next model: Horst Buchholz, an actor who became famous at a very young age. He was working here with many other actors who I recognized from their movies, and I met all of them. Again, I had to sit behind the scenery and model while the shooting of the movie was in progress. I immediately established a very good relationship with Horst Buchholz. He came over to me right away during every recess, and we found a quiet corner where he posed patiently. Working with him was a pleasure, and we soon had a personal bond between us.

I was busy modeling in the various movie studios for the next few weeks; there was almost always tension in the air, as is only natural in that industry. I met many interesting people. Top performances were expected from all involved, especially from the actors. Every minute was costly, and therefore, working hours didn't adhere to a regular schedule. I saw at the time that fame has its price: Aside from the satisifying and pleasant aspects of it, there also were a great many disadvantages! I didn't realize it then, but I would experience some of that in the future. (Many decades later, in 1993, an article was published about these movie-star dolls in the German doll collectors' magazine, *Cièslik's Puppen Magazine*.)

An Artist's Excursions

1957 and 1959

There it was, the masterpiece of Michelangelo Buonaroti. I had dreamed about it often; I had looked at it many times in art books or on the postcards that my mother had sent me many years before. Now I was standing in front of it and the reality was overwhelming. No photograph, no matter how excellent, could reflect the impression that emanated from these marble statues. Here in the sanctuary of St. Lorenzo in Florence, Italy, I spent a long time admiring the burial sites of the Medici. I also was deeply moved by the giant David. It was only years later, during one of many trips with my wife Sieglinde, that I admired the other works of this great Renaissance master.

In 1957, during the Easter break, I went to Italy, my second trip there, with a travel group from the high school in Coburg, under the guidance of an art historian. After crossing the Alps by bus, we arrived at Lake Garda. It was here, in Riva, that I saw a typical Italian landscape for the first time, with its flat-roofed houses and cypress trees. Until then, I had only seen postcards of this scenery. The deep blue sky, the deep blue water and the spring blossoms were enchanting. This trip brought us to many prominent northern Italian cities, from Verona via Padua and Venice, to Ravenna. These places, filled with famous art treasures, left a lasting impression on all of us.

A year before, I had seen a short newspaper article about an art-history trip to Holland during the Rembrandt anniversary. With article in hand, I went to Franz Goebel and received his permission to take this trip with my colleague, Menzenbach. Goebel would pay for our

70

expenses. With a group of art aficionados from Coburg, we traveled the length and breadth of Holland for two weeks, visiting all the important museums and landmarks. We admired the famous Dutch school paintings, especially those of Rembrandt (who is my favorite painter) and those of Rubens and many others. I had seen many of these famous paintings while visiting art galleries in Berlin, but the greatest number and the most important of them were to be seen in Holland.

I took a number of art appreciation tours throughout Europe over the years, such as one to the Brussels World Fair in 1958 and a year later, one to Paris, where I went to the Louvre to view its unparalleled collection of art. On future trips, whether they were for business or for pleasure, I seized the opportunity to visit museums and art exhibits. With my wife Sieglinde, I have traveled to historic spots in all corners of the world. I think that it widens our scope and deepens our appreciation for the cultural and artistic achievements of mankind. Moreover, you develop a greater tolerance towards other peoples and their cultures.

One special trip remains a vivid memory. A total eclipse of the sun was predicted for Europe on February 15, 1961, the center of which would be directly over Florence. With my background in astronomy, I was very, very interested in this event, especially since the next total eclipse would not occur until 1999; however, I wasn't able to find the money for such a journey. So I went to Franz Goebel and explained my travel plans, suggesting that I also might visit a number of places in Italy that contained art treasures. He immediately agreed and, to my great surprise, offered me the use of one of his private cars. As he handed me the car keys, he pointed to the gold keychain and said, "If you run out of money, you can always hock this." That wasn't necessary, as it turned out.

I spent several days in Florence, where there was a lot to see. This city in Tuscany, with its indescribable artistic ambiance, has a special place in my heart, and I couldn't resist spending a few days there whenever I was in the area. I arose very early on the day of the eclipse and drove into the Tuscany mountains so that I would get a good spot with unrestricted vision towards the east. Thousands of people were on the road in cars and buses to witness this rare occurrence. I found a very suitable position on a plateau facing east and overlooking a valley. I set up my telescope and wide-angle camera because I wanted to photograph the progression of the eclipse in a series of pictures. The people around me must have thought I was a professional, with all my equipment, because I got all the room I needed, and everybody was interested in my preparations.

It was a beautiful spring morning, and when the sun rose, the birds started singing, as they usually did at that time of day. But then the moon slowly began to move in front of the sun, and the eclipse, even though not yet noticeable around us, had started. I shot the first picture in my series of the eclipse and through my telescope, I could see the mountainous rim of the moon in front of the sun. Slowly, the moon moved further, covering more and more of the sun's disc. The brightness of the morning gave way to a very pale light; it grew darker. The birds stopped singing, and it felt as if all of nature were holding its breath. Then, just before the last ray of sunlight disappeared behind the moon, the moon's shadow raced across the horizon in a crimson hue, and blanketed the whole area around us, darkening everything. A cold wind sent shivers up my spine and an ominous darkness settled on the earth with a depressing atmosphere. At the edge of the darkened sun, though, the corona was illuminated in a display of indescribable beauty. Soon, the first sun ray reappeared, it began to get lighter, and slowly nature seemed to awaken from its sleep. The air became warmer and soon the birds started chirping again. This left a deep impression on me, and I began to understand ancient man's fear of such a total eclipse.

Sickness
1959

A week had gone by since I had been admitted to the hospital in Coburg. I shared a large room with three other patients of various ages on the ward for internal medicine. I really felt miserable. The doctors took samples of gastric fluids through a tube that I had to swallow. Sitting behind an X-ray machine, I had to swallow a special mush that tasted like plaster of Paris, and a nurse took blood at certain intervals. In short, I was caught in the relentless grip of a hospital examination, and there was no escape. My personal physician of many years, Dr. Fichte, who had treated me for gastritis, had me admitted to the hospital for a thorough battery of tests. She suspected, not without cause, that I had developed an ulcer and, most likely, an inflammation of the liver. With mixed feelings, I now awaited the results of these tests.

The day before, I had visited an older fellow patient in the "death chamber," as it was commonly called by the patients and the hospital personnel. He was a forester by profession, and during an extended patrol through the forest, had suffered severe frostbite on his right foot. The foot became gangrenous, he got blood poisoning, and his leg had to be amputated. The amputation was too late, though; the gangrene had spread throughout his body, and he was dying. It is not an easy task to comfort a dying person, but I tried nonetheless, since there was nobody else to take care of him. The nurses only administered painkillers because he could not be helped any more; most likely, his medical file had already been closed. He was conscious and alert. Our conversation revolved around the subject that worries a dying person the most: What comes after death? Even though the forester was somewhat apprehensive, he seemed surprisingly composed and did not rail at his impending death. The hours I spent with the dying man clearly showed me how little thought we devote to our own mortality, in the daily bustle of our lives. A young person, especially, tries to push aside any thought of the inevitable, which seems far away and remote. The next day, the forester was gone—he had died during the night.

A few days after this, I had an appointment with the medical chief, Dr. Diezel, who gave me the results of my tests in a fatherly way. My physical condition was not good: Besides having extensive stomach ulcers, the inflammation of the liver also was confirmed. Medication and a very strict diet might improve my condition to an extent, but I would probably need to have surgery. Then the doctor asked me if I were under any stress or had any emotional problems, since this can often cause such illness. I discussed my marital problems and my struggle to advance my career with him. My physical resistance against this double assault was not strong enough in the long run. The consultation with this experienced physician made it clear to me that I had to change my life completely if I hoped to regain my health as well as my professional achievements.

While convalescing for a few weeks in Bad Kissingen, a health spa, I found myself far removed from the daily problems of life, and had ample time to consider my current situation. At the spa, I learned to discipline myself and to live on a very strict diet. I ate dairy products almost exclusively, and drank no alcohol. At the end of my convalescence, I came to the conclusion that I had to get a divorce. That was the only way I could redirect my life and give it new meaning. Once back home, I attended a course under the direction of Dr. Fichte that consisted of relaxation exercises and I followed my diet rigidly. Slowly, my physical condition began to improve, as did my career. Franz Goebel and the sisters at the Siessen Convent accepted me as the successor to Mr. Unger and Mr. Moeller, both of whom had been dominant forces in the creation of the M.I. Hummel figurines. All of this contributed to the gradual improvement of my health, without an operation, and I looked forward to the future with renewed hope.

Never Again
1962

Everything went smoothly at our divorce hearing. The judge asked a few questions, which were answered either by us or by our attorney. Basically, the questions concerned the legal custody of the children. Then came the judgement: "I hereby declare this marriage dissolved!"

As I walked down the steps of the circuit court in Coburg, I felt as if a huge burden had been lifted from my shoulders. A part of my life, which had begun so promisingly, had ended abruptly. After 15 years of marriage, it had been no easy decision to ask for divorce. Our two daughters would suffer the most from this separation, but I could see no other solution than to end a marriage that had existed only on paper for the past few years. We had agreed to part harmoniously to keep court and legal fees within reasonable limits. Since the value of the existing property was negligible, the welfare of our children was our main concern. My now ex-wife planned to remarry right after the divorce and would be well taken care of. We agreed that each of us should take custody of one of our daughters: my ex-wife would take nine-year-old Victoria and I would take 15-year-old Suzanne. This day of finality caused fundamental changes in all of our lives.

It is not very easy to write about the defeats and set-backs in your life, and a shattered marriage is definitely a set-back—it's a breakdown of a relationship. The blame very seldom rests on one partner; almost always, it's both who contribute to such a failure, be it through attitude, misunderstandings, or drastically different beliefs and interests.

I stayed by myself in our apartment after my ex-wife moved out and married an acquaintance. Suzanne had been living at her boarding school for some time, primarily due to school-related problems most likely brought on by the unhappy situation at home. I was firmly resolved never to marry again; perhaps I was not suited for a partnership.

During these years as a single male in the prime of life living in a large apartment, I had, after a lengthy abstinence, several relationships with the opposite sex. But I always broke them off as soon as they threatened to become serious. Together with a circle of "imbibing" friends, I held many parties in my apartment or in cozy country inns around Coburg. But, in the long run, I wasn't very satisfied with this kind of lifestyle, even though many of my married friends envied me. I began to wonder more and more often whether this self-imposed "never again" attitude of mine was really a final decision for the second half of my life that still lay ahead.

Never Say "Never Again"
1964–1965

For more than two hours we had been sitting in the Palace wine cellar in Wuerzburg; we only had eyes for each other. We were a little surprised and embarrassed when suddenly my friend Georg got up and said huffily, "I can see that you do not need me any longer and so I am going home!" We had completely forgotten about him. And really, we should have been very grateful to him because he was the one who introduced us.

I had been friends with Georg for many years, and we had taken many local trips together in the Coburg area. One day he mentioned to me that he had met a very appealing girl—even her size was right for me. Because I was short, I always had problems with women, so her height interested me. Then he showed me a photograph of a very beautiful girl with a very self-confident look on her face. If I were interested, he said condescendingly, he could arrange a rendezvous. The result was this memorable first meeting with my future wife, Sieglinde. From the very first moment, we got along and found out that we had many mutual interests. We grew fonder of each other. Then, finally, this embarrassing situation with Georg happened. After we apologized and talked him into staying, the three of us had a very pleasant evening together. I was on fire, though, and Sieglinde agreed to another date with me. I drove home to Coburg, feeling somewhat dubious. Had my resolve never to marry again not been a bit hasty?

When I returned from a business trip, we began to spend every weekend together. Most of the time I drove to Wuerzburg, where we scouted out the most romantic wineries in the area. On Friday evenings, arriving in Wuerzburg after a week of hard work, I would find Sieglinde busily preparing a tasty supper for me. She, who had never any interest in cooking at all, created one gourmet meal after another, and all week long, I looked forward to my trip to Wuerzburg. Then Sieglinde visited me in Coburg, where I not only showed her the sights of the city, but introduced her to my friends. A hiking trip through the Spessart mountains for several days and a trip on a sailship to the coastal islands of Yugoslavia brought us closer together, and I thought about marrying her. Although she liked me very much, too, marriage would not be as simple as we thought. Sieglinde had a very good job as head secretary in a very large bank, and it would not be easy for her to give up her independence.

Sieglinde was an exceptional gymnast, as well as a glider pilot, fencer, skier and sailor. This impressed me very much. She was an accomplished equestrienne and diver, but she also loved to hike through the countryside and the forests. I could barely stop her from skydiving! With the exception of fencing and piloting gliders (our son Martin is now an accomplished glider pilot), we shared an interest in these sports and did them together. And so it happened that we became engaged during a ski holiday in the Bavarian Alps on New Year's Eve 1964. Our great love for each other and our many mutual interests finally convinced Sieglinde that we should spend the rest of our lives together. Boredom didn't have a chance in our lives! I was welcomed with open arms by her parents, and spent many happy hours with her family.

Finally, the great day arrived. On September 2, 1965, we were married, and celebrated our wedding at a small, but very lively party in Coburg. Afterwards, we took off for a sea-diving expedition on the island of Elba in the Mediterranean Sea. This small island is famous, not only as the location of Napoleon's first exile, but as a diving mecca because of its exceptionally clear waters. En route, we visited several famous Italian cities, Pisa, Verona and of course, Florence. As an artist, I appreciated the latter city the most, and we spent several days there taking in all the sights and the art. We stayed in an old palace, a really romantic spot for honeymooners! Once on Elba, we attended a two-week course in sea-diving and experienced for the first time the fantastic underwater world, which, with the help of scuba equipment, we could explore at our leisure. The only set-back was that Sieglinde came down with an ear infection and couldn't finish the course. I became so fascinated with the underwater world that it continues to hold me. (Later, I was able to use what I had learned and seen while diving in my work, modeling various types of fish for Goebel.) I had built my first underwater camera by myself, making a pressure-proof resin housing for my Contax camera. I could then preserve our diving experiences for posterity.

When we returned from our honeymoon. Sieglinde and I enthusiastically started to refurbish our living quarters. Since we both loved antiques, we began buying old furniture as cheaply as possible and learned how to restore the pieces ourselves. While I was busy with the wooden parts, reshaping missing pieces, Sieglinde scraped and polished the old furniture following the tradition of the old craftsmen. We installed new floors and added beams to the ceiling of our dining room (which was dubbed the "Knight's Hall" by our friends because of its decorating style). Our living quarters were in a mansion-like house that was built in 1871; after our children arrived, we were constantly rearranging everything. If we found a very special, valuable piece of furniture on one of our trips, it might happen that we would replace an existing piece of furniture with a new "old" one.

Camping and Sailing
Summer 1966

The first spat of our married life began in the middle of a lake, in our brand-new boat. Sieglinde, the accomplished sailor, tried to teach me the very strict rules of sailing. Apparently, I was a very stubborn student. Anyway, she tried to tell me that the pulley by which the main sail is hoisted up the mast was attached to the wrong side of the mast. I was of the opinion that it didn't matter on which side of the mast it was fastened, but Sieglinde insisted that the correct fastening was of great importance, in case we needed to make a sudden maneuver. With my growing experience as a sailor, I finally gave in and followed her rules precisely—it just takes time to learn everything!

The water above and below the surface fascinated us so much that we bought a seagoing rubber dinghy. Since the use of outboard motors is prohibited on most German lakes, ours was equipped with both sails and motor. This way, we could use it on a nice little lake near Coburg when we were not on vacation somewhere else. So we spent the summer weekends in a small tent on the camping grounds adjacent to this little lake, feeling as if we were in the middle of nature. Our camping gear consisted of only the bare necessities, and I had made most of them myself. In order to save space, everything had to be foldable to fit in our Volkswagen Beetle. A luggage carrier on the roof of the car held the larger boat sections and the tent, but everything else had to fit in the back of the car, where I had removed the seats. We went on vacation like this to France, Spain or Italy. One day, our neighbor, who had been watching us stow all our equipment into that little car, made no bones about it—the car would break down right outside of Coburg. To reassure him, we later sent him a card from the Spanish Costa Brava!

During our third year of marriage, we took an especially memorable trip to Sicily. The tent stayed home because we planned to stay in a hotel on the island of Vulkano, which is in the Aolien Islands, north of Sicily. Since the Autostrada del Sol was only finished as far as Naples in 1967, we had to travel through the Appenines on steep mountainside roads with hairpin curves. The Volkswagen "bug" proved itself on this leg of the trip, mastering the mountain roads effortlessly with its small, 35-horsepower engine despite all of our heavy luggage. When we reached the port of Milazzo, we had to unload the car, leave it there, and get all of our gear—suitcases, boat parts, motor, masts, canisters, diving gear and many other things—onto the ferry that would take us to our destination. There were a lot of seasick passengers on board because the weather was stormy, and there were further delays: a large cargo of pigs had to be taken to the south coast of Vulcano. Small boats were used to transfer them to shore, so we didn't arrive at the port until after nightfall. Our ship had to stay outside the harbor; we were put onto flat-bottomed boats that took us to the port. As I stood on the pier and in the fading light, watched the transfer of all our possessions onto a boat, I swore that we would never see any of it again. But—lo and behold—not a single piece was missing when we piled everything on top of an old truck for the trip to the hotel.

In Vulcano—the word "volcano" comes from this island—I discovered my interest in studying volcanic eruptions. We scaled Mount Aetna, Europe's largest active volcano, which was very impressive, and we stayed overnight at the volcanological observatory, 7,000 feet up the mountain (today, it is buried under 100 feet of lava). We watched a beautiful sunset while the crater spewed fountains of lava into the sky. Early the next morning, we went up the other side of the huge volcano and saw a stream of glowing lava flowing downhill. Ever since, I have been fascinated by live volcanos.

Camping in our tent worked out very well—that is, until the big thunderstorm. It was a very humid summer day. We had erected our tent in a clearing, since that was the only place where we could find a breeze. During the night, a very heavy thunderstorm arose; it swept through the clearing with great force. Our tent started to lift up, and we had to hold it down by the metal rods. Heavy rains poured down and lightning struck all around us. Potatoes and tomatoes rolled around inside the tent, and we had our hands full to keep the tent from flying away. The thought of lightning hitting the metal tent rods was not very comforting. After this ordeal was over, we decided to buy a small camper. Since the bug wasn't really built to pull such a large load, we decided to buy a larger car, too.

It's not very easy to guide a 12-foot trailer through the very narrow streets of Europe. You need a lot of experience to park such a long rig and to move it in reverse. One time, Sieglinde had a funny feeling while I was maneuvering the rig in the mountains, so we decided to get out of the car and have a look. To our horror, we discovered that the back end of the trailer was hanging over a steep cliff, the depth of which we couldn't even guess. If I had backed up only a few inches more, the trailer would have yanked us down into an abyss! Throughout our marriage, I have often admired Sieglinde's ability to sense danger; apparently, this talent is hidden somewhere in the female psyche. We males, with our more rational way of thinking, can't compete with this natural instinct.

With our ability to handle a sailboat growing, we needed something more challenging. Our cumbersome dinghy didn't satisfy us anymore; we wanted a real sailboat or a yacht. After an extensive search, we purchased a yawl. It was a very nice boat, large enough to accommodate a growing family, yet small enough to fit on the roof of our car, barely. With this yawl—I still own an exact duplicate of the first one—we took many voyages on the sea, as well as on our little lake. All of our vacations were spent at the seashore or at large lakes in southern Europe. From the time they were born, both our sons, Martin and Stephan, had contact with the water. Later on, we added surfing to our repertoire, a sport in which Martin excelled. When the waves grew bigger and bigger during stormy weather, and most surfers went back to shore, he would surf out to sea at a breathtaking speed. Sieglinde and I both appreciate the challenge of water and wind, and experience a feeling of freedom and joy when our well-trimmed boat races smoothly across the raging waves. But we enjoy a silent sail under a light breeze right before sundown, too. A romantic, almost dreamlike atmosphere prevails during these evening sails, and at these times, far from my studio, I have been inspired to think of ideas for new sculptures.

A Sudden Death and a Great Loss
July 1969

There was going to be a big celebration when Franz Goebel reached his 65th birthday two days hence. Preparations were in high gear; every day, new guests from around the world arrived in Roedental. For generations, company parties had been a tradition at Goebel, and despite the ever-increasing number of employees, these affairs were still like family parties. There was a very festive atmosphere at the main factory and also at the branch factories; everyone looked forward to the big company festival with music and dancing, food and drink and many other attractions.

Then the news struck like a bolt of lightening: Franz Goebel was dead! Two days before his birthday, he suffered a fatal heart attack in the garden of his house, which was next to the factory. Joy gave way to shock and despair. On everyone's face, you could see the nagging question: "What's going to happen now?" I, too, was deeply affected by this event. When I heard the sad news, I immediately began to sculpt a bust of Franz Goebel. Only the day before, I had had a meeting with him, and I wanted to sculpt him as he lived in my memory. This work was to be my final thanks to a great human being, a man to whom I felt very loyal and to whom I was grateful for many things. I worked all week long on this bust; I showed it to members of the family for their comments and approval before making a plaster-of-Paris mold from which several casts could be made. The bust was later exhibited in the company's information center and also in the Franz Goebel Hall. I was asked by Wilhlem Goebel to make

83

the same portrait in bronze relief for the family gravesite in front of the Goebel house.

Instead of the planned celebration, a large funeral procession escorted Franz Goebel to his final resting place. He was very, very popular with the employees, our "Goebel Family," especially for his efforts towards the social advancement among the workers; it would be no easy task for his successor to bridge the gap. But life goes on, and his son, Wilhelm Goebel, with the support of his uncle, Dr. Eux Stocke and his cousin, Utz Stocke, took over the reins of the company. After a period of transition and a number of changes, a new style of leadership emerged. The creation of a modern management team was followed by years of expansion and diversification. Through the expansion of the entire product line, the M.I. Hummel figurines were pushed into the background a bit, but always remained the most important part of production. I created many new figurines, and the meetings with representatives of the Siessen Convent continued. The new management escalated efforts to reach and maintain a high standard of quality. The new team also worked constantly on the modernization of production facilities and processes.

For all the employees who knew Franz Goebel or worked closely with him, there remains the lasting memory of an unusual man who created his own lasting monument with the introduction of the Hummel figurines.

Martin and Stephan

August 1969 and April 1972

A lively party was in swing on our small balcony high above the city of Coburg on a Sunday in August 1969. My two friends, the brothers Georg and Gerhard, were helping me celebrate the birth of our first son, Martin. Both of them had recently become fathers of sons, and we celebrated this triple event lavishly. Again and again, we toasted our wives and our sons, sang old songs, and were up to a lot of nonsense and mischief. Another old friend of ours, Klaus the pharmacist, had mixed a batch of black powder according to an old recipe. We loaded the barrels of my antique muskets with this stuff (without bullets, of course), and shot off a booming salute. We were very lucky that these guns, which were several hundred years old, didn't explode on us, but a man will do a lot of silly things when a son and heir arrives! We sang a lot of wild songs, and stuck the old blunderbusses through the openings of the balcony railing, taking aim at the Department of Forestry building across the street. To this day, I am still surprised that nobody lodged a complaint. They probably all accepted the fact that new fathers do behave oddly. Why is that, I wonder. Is it because they see themselves in their new sons or is it just the old societal tradition of valuing sons more than daughters? It was probably both reasons that made us so giddy and frolicsome. In the meanwhile, our son was sleeping in the arms of his very happy mother.

I was not allowed to attend the real reason for this party, the birth of the child. The physicians and midwives were adamantly opposed to having the father present at the birth. One of their arguments was that men have weak stomachs. They knew of cases where the attending physician or midwife had to take care of a fainting father rather than tending to the mother-to-be. But when the time approached for the birth of our second son, Stephan, I was stubborn and insisted on being there. I have strong nerves, and it was reassuring to Sieglinde to have me by her side. When she was ready, I drove her to the hospital, donned a white smock and took her up to the delivery room. The midwife, who had been attending another birth, arrived only after the head of the child had already crowned. Sieglinde held onto my hand firmly while I talked to her soothingly. Then the door opened, and a doctor in a white smock entered. He looked at me and said, "Ah, my colleague is already here," and started to leave. "Stop!" I called out to him. "Stay here! I am only the father!" He had mistook me, dressed in a white smock, for another doctor; we had to laugh about the mix-up.

The birth of a new human being is a very impressive thing; my advice to any father is to be present if at all possible. Two people who have created this new being should be together when it is born.

The Big Merry Wanderer
1968–1971

Some time before his death, Franz Goebel had summoned me to his office. "Sit down," he said. "I have something very important to discuss with you." In his paternal tone and with an air of secrecy, he continued, "But this has to remain between us." Then he let me in on his idea: "For a long time now, I have thought of erecting an oversize M.I. Hummel figurine in front of the factory. A good occasion for doing this would be the 100th anniversary of the company in 1971, three years from now." Then he added that, in his opinion, such a large figurine could only be cast in concrete. I disagreed: "Since we are a well-known porcelain factory, we should create such a large figurine from weatherproof ceramic material; we owe that to our image, in my opinion." When he shook his head in dissent, I reminded him of the oversize ceramic figurines in China along the burial lanes, about which I only knew from the books I had read. Franz Goebel continued to have his doubts, and summoned our technical director, Mr. Litzow. When I had presented my plan, he wagged his head in a calculating way, meaning "it is not altogether impossible, what you have in mind." But first we would have to develop a weatherproof ceramic, and then we would have to put it to the test through at least one winter. We would also need a weather-resistant paint for this type of climate, and our current colors, which were used for the final glaze, would not do. Only color glazing combined with proper under- and inner-glazing colors could be used. Since we needed only one figurine for this purpose, it was my intention to construct it from mal-

87

leable material that could be fired, without the benefit of a mold. I was willing to take the risk that I would have to reshape the entire figurine from scratch should damage occur along the way. So, we agreed to develop a suitable material in our own laboratory, and create and decorate larger objects that could be exposed to the weather. We were able very quickly to make several thick-walled vases and an oversize candelabra from the test material as planned, and we set them up in the Goebel garden. (I still have one of these experimental vases, done in the faience technique, standing in my hallway at home.)

Time passed, and all the test pieces withstood the onslaught of winter, and were really weatherproof. Due to the death of Franz Goebel and the subsequent company reorganization, more than a year passed before I had a meeting with Wilhelm Goebel about this project. The Merry Wanderer, in the meantime, had become a kind of symbol for the company, and its compact nature made it very suitable for my purpose. Wilhelm Goebel agreed to my plans and commissioned me to start on the project.

For starters, I had the craftsmen at the factory construct a large turntable with a three-foot diameter on which I could erect the figurine, making it possible for me to swivel it around in order to work on it from all sides. From the clay mill at the factory, I ordered 2,500 pounds of the special weatherproof material. It had to "sit" for several weeks to improve its pliability. Finally, the day came when I could begin this enormous project.

Never before had such a large ceramic figurine been created at the Goebel factory, and most experts probably thought of my endeavor as being utopian, destined to end in failure. I, however, was completely convinced that I could accomplish my goal, but because I lacked experience in making such a large object, had to think every step through. I was certain that the figurine could not be solid, not only because of the weight, but because of the problems in firing it. I found the ideal solution for the inner structure of the figurine in nature itself: the cellular structure of plants, where the inner walls were connected through openings. This was the only way that I was able to achieve an optimal stability and a relatively light weight. This system, however, required from the beginning very strict adherence to the proportions. Later corrections would only be possible to a very, very limited extent. Since the largest Merry Wanderer in current production, Hummel 7/III, was really very small in comparison to my project, I decided to create an interim model of about three feet. This would be a tremendous help in transferring the correct proportions to the large figurine. I had not expected that this intermediate Merry Wanderer would be put into production as Hummel 7/X, and we did have a lot of problems with the firing process.

When all the basic preparations were finished, I could begin the monumental task at hand. The turntable had been insulated with metal foil. My apprentice had thoroughly kneaded the special material, and I started by forming the base or postament, as we called it. Next, I molded the shoes. The big lumps of clay, each weighing more than two pounds, had to be well integrated: there could be no air blisters or cracks during the modeling process, since they would lead to larger fissures at firing time. I had calculated everything precisely. The thickness of the walls had to be greater at the bottom, and would become gradually thinner towards the top. After I had molded the outlines of the huge shoes—they looked like an antique excavation site—I started having doubts. Had I bitten off more than I could chew? After all, there is a big difference between having an idea and making it a reality. But there was no backing out now. I cast my doubts aside, and my optimism again won the upper hand. I continued with my work.

Slowly, the legs with their intra-cell structure grew upwards, and I did not have to bend down anymore, as in the beginning. Quitting time came, and my assistant, Jochen Bauer (today a member of our modeling team), went home while I worked a little longer. Suddenly, I realized that the right leg, on which I was working, had started to move, and threatened to fall over! In the process, it started to drag the other leg down, too. Apparently, the modeling mass that I was using had been too soft. I braced both legs with my shoulder, thinking that there was no way that I could build a support by myself while I was in this position. The right leg had already lost its shape, so I decided to at least save the left leg. I looked for my large knife, and spotted it on the ground, a few yards away. I raced over to the knife, grabbed it and cut the slowly sinking right leg off. It fell into a heap with a muffled thud. Then I built a supporting scaffolding around the left leg. I got home late that night, but all the work had not been in vain. The next morning, as I was busy modeling a new leg, the company architect came to visit me. When he realized what kind of dimensions this figurine would have, he asked me what its total weight would be. I answered, "About 3,300 pounds." He thought about that for a moment, and then took a piece of paper and started to calculate. His final conclusion was that all rooms under my studio, down to the basement, had to be shored up. The old building could not carry such a load, and with a few visitors standing around the figurine, everything could collapse. Consequently, the company carpenters arrived early the next morning and installed props and supports directly under the figurine in all three rooms below the studio.

During the work on this colossal piece, we faced, time and again, new and unforeseen problems; but we mastered them all. Then came the day when the figurine was finally finished; Wilhelm Goebel came over with his staff of executives to inspect it. Every last one of them was impressed. But then, Wilhelm Goebel looked at the entranceway and asked me, "How in the world are you going to get this figurine through that door?" The door opening was really much lower, but I could put his mind at ease. For firing purposes alone, the figurine would have to be cut into several sections, and after the glazing process, the individual parts would be rejoined with cement in their respective locations. This all sounds so easy, but we encountered new problems when cutting the still-soft material into the projected sections. Many strong men were needed to lift the heavy parts, and I held my breath several times. But everything did go well. Because of the thickness of the figurine's walls, it had to dry for many weeks, and had to be fired very slowly. I supervised the entire operation, watching like a hawk that everything was done according to plan. Even a small mistake could ruin the entire project.

The glaze was sprayed on after the first firing, and Guenter Neubauer painted all parts with the specially prepared faience colors. He had to be extremely careful because the paint could not be erased once it was applied or the glaze, which was only dried and not fired, would have been wiped off, too. Since faience colors, which are destined for high-temperature firings, have only a very limited spectrum, it was not an easy task to create the correct shades that are used in painting the Hummel figurines. Finally, we were ready. We started to erect the huge figurine in front of the factory, shielded and protected by a tent that was open at the top. Again, we had a number of problems. On several parts, I had to make corrections with a heavy chisel, so that they would fit together properly. Some pieces, such as arms and legs, were wrapped with stainless-steel wires in order to give the figurine more stability. We finished just in time for the big occasion, the 100th anniversary of the Goebel company.

The unveiling was a great event for employees and guests alike. The main road from Coburg to Roedental was completely blocked off for more than an hour to accommodate the 2,000-plus people who attended the unveiling. When Wilhelm Goebel and Utz Stocke pulled the cover away from the statue, an admiring "Ahhh" arose from the crowd standing tightly packed on the road outside the factory. During the festivities that followed on the factory grounds, I was congratulated many times for my achievement in creating a very visible landmark for the Goebel company. The only sad note was that Franz Goebel was not around to see the realization of his idea. But I am sure that he would have approved of it wholeheartedly.

Volcanos

May 1971, January 1973, May 1987

MOUNT AETNA

When I climbed Mount Aetna a few years ago, I did not realize how soon I would again be attracted to this mountain. But this time, it was completely different. This volcano had been active again for many weeks, and it had one of the greatest eruptions in centuries. With my friends Helmut and Klaus—one a physician and the other a pharmacist—I followed every bit of news about it in the media. One day, we all decided to see the eruptions with our own eyes. Equipped with cameras, film and even spare rations, we started out on the 36-hour train ride to Sicily—one of my most memorable and eventful trips.

From far away, we could already see the column of smoke that erupted from the crest of the mountain. We rode by bus from Catania to the mountain villages in the higher regions, where we were able to find a place to stay. There, we had the great fortune of meeting Franz Lazi, a famous director and producer of nature movies from Stuttgart. He was there to take action pictures for German television. Since his assistant had to fly back home to Stuttgart, he readily accepted our offer to help him in his venture; he took us along in his rental car, and we tried to get as close to the crest as possible. But suddenly, there was a roadblock, and the police guarding it would not let a single car past that point. However, when we showed them the large television camera and shouted, "Televisione Tedesco!" they let us pass through. The final destination was the "Refugio Sapinza," a sort of mountaintop refuge and inn located at an altitude of almost 6,000 feet. (We had to transfer to a jeep, since the cable lift that went to the plateau at the peak, which was 9,000 feet high, had been destroyed by the lava flow.) We continued our exhausting ascent by foot, climbing tediously over bizarre lava-mass shapes. These masses were still warm; only a foot and a half beneath our feet lay glowing, red-hot lava. One slip of the foot would have been fatal. A muffled grumbling arose, the whole mountain trembled, and we were greeted by a thunderous roar and a tremendous eruption of the new crater, which was located right in front of us. Black ash, white water and fountains of steam, and large rocks were projected several hundred yards in the air. The descending rocks kept us at bay. We photographed and filmed continuously but when the eruption intensified and large chunks of rock began falling around us, we had to retreat. It was nightfall before we left this fascinating scenery and made our way back to the inn. That evening, we discussed our unprecedented experience over a pizza and Sicilian wine.

Streams of lava had blocked almost all the streets, and we had to make a lot of detours the next day on our way to the "Bocen," the "gateway to hell." We proceeded over steep forest roads—at times, pushing the car—until it was impossible to go any further. Again, we had to grope our way across strange lava deposits, loaded down with heavy backpacks, film, cameras and tripods, as well as our sleeping bags and provisions. In the midst of a forest 6,000 feet up, the earth had opened to reveal an inferno. It was already dark when we got there, and we found billowing clouds of poisonous gases. A pulp of molten rock, more than 1,000 degrees centigrade, shot up from fissures in the ground and rumbled downhill, bubbling and roaring ominously. From one of these "boccas," the mountain spewed lava so forcefully that slivers flew all around us, and we had to take cover repeatedly. The fire stream cascaded vertically into a ravine from where it flowed down into the valley, making its own pathway directly next to us. The poisonous gases impaired our breathing. It was not too hard to imagine that this could have been the entrance to Hell! This impression grew with the impending darkness. We ascended further up the mountain and finally stood atop the largest bocca. The fire stream flowed out of the mountain directly below us. From this vantage point, we could also see the other lava streams, which looked like the fiery tentacles of a giant squid, destroying everything in their paths down to the valleys below. We decided to spend the night here, at the entrance of Hades. Stretched out on the black lava-sand, kept warm and illuminated by one of the greatest of nature's spectacles, we hardly slept a wink.

The following morning, we wanted to return to our quarters in the village of Zafferana, but we got only as far as the bridge of Fornazzo. A huge crowd had gathered there, watching with excitement a large stream of lava that crept downhill in a dry riverbed. This glowing stream, which contained larger rocks already somewhat cooled, was now of a thicker consistency and thus slower, having run a course of several miles. The air was filled with a noise that sounded like thousands of crickets, caused by the cooling and shrinking lava. The heat scorched all the trees and shrubs in a wide area. From the curling leaves to the largest branches, a trembling and moaning sound emanated from the dying trees. They looked like giant torches before being swallowed up by the fiery stream. Like an enormous dragon, this stream pushed relentlessly toward the bridge, which it reached at the beginning of nightfall. A cry went up from the crowd as a large piece of lava rock demolished the stone railing of the bridge. It looked like a big oven, when the glowing magma pressed through the arch of the bridge while a mountain of lava, which had piled up to a height of more than 30 feet, finally buried the bridge under its mass. In the meantime, the inhabitants of the neighboring village gathered up all of their belongings that could be moved: windows and doors were removed, the wine was pumped out of cellars, and furniture loaded on trucks. Only the skeletons of their houses remained. All this was done with an unbelievable calmness by these people who had lived for centuries under the threat of the volcano. They prayed and did not give up hope that the lava stream would miss their houses.

HEIMAEY

It happened again two years later. But this time, the earth burst open in the north, near the Arctic Circle. The island of Heimaey lies eight miles off the coast of southern Iceland, which is known for its fertile fishing grounds. On this island is the volcano Helgafell, which had been dormant for more than 5,000 years. The harbor, protected by a 600-foot-high mountainside, had been ideally suited for the establishment of an extensive fish canning industry. Here, next to the town of Vestmannaeyjar, home of this industry, the earth erupted on the night of January 22, 1973. During this eruption, the noise of it awakening the whole town, the island was split in two. More than 40 lava cascades, almost 5,000 feet long, burst skywards and then dropped into the boiling sea. A rain of volcanic ashes descended on the entire town. In a lightening-like response, the 5,000-plus inhabitants were evacuated to a safer place by the fishing fleet, which just happened to be anchored in the harbor. This was followed by the evacuation of cars, livestock, furniture and the inventory of the canneries to the Iceland mainland.

When I heard the first reports of this eruption over the radio, I did not hesitate long; the next morning I was sitting on an airplane with my friend Helmut, well-equipped and ready for this event. Aboard the Icelandair flight, we met Mr. Lagerkranz, editor in chief of *Dagens Nyheter*, the largest newspaper in Sweden. He was also travelling to Heimaey to see the new volcano. At the Hotel Borg in Reykjavik, we met several other journalists who had no idea of how we could get to the island, which had been declared off limits. We finally decided to follow the advice of a Danish correspondent, to try to get there by boat. We drove in a taxi through the countryside, beautifully illuminated by the aurora borealis, to the port of Thorlakshoevn, located on the southern coast. Mr. Lagerkranz proved to be an expert on Iceland and entertained us with stories about this interesting land. The only signs of life that we encountered over seemingly endless white stretches of land were ravens, the holy birds of Iceland. Then, we got a big break: The captain of a small fishing trawler used in the rescue operation agreed to take us along; he stubbornly refused any payment for his services. In the ensuing days, we would have many more opportunities to appreciate the hospitality of the Icelandic people.

The heavy seas rolled the trawler from one side to the other for three and a half hours; I felt like I was dying. But my seasickness vanished when I saw the huge cloud of smoke and ashes that extended like a pillar from the earth to sky, seeming to support the heavens. As a sort of infernal greeting, the new volcano spewed a series of fiery cascades into the air, accompanied by a resounding hiss. A broad stream of lava was rolling downhill from the mountain, and poured into the boiling, hissing sea. Dense white clouds of steam enveloped our ship as we made our way to the harbor entrance, sailing very close to the steep rock formations.

The lava stream had created a new land mass. In just a few days, it built up an area almost a square mile from an ocean depth of 120 feet. The lava mass, with a temperature of 900 degrees centigrade, could have devastating consequences for the rich fishing grounds by warming up the surrounding waters too quickly.

Appalled by the destruction, yet expectant, we entered Vestmannaeyjar, which only a few days before had been a lively, booming industrial town. Now, the streets were deserted and everything was covered by a layer of black ash. We put on our safety helmets and started on our way to the volcano. Every so often, we would encounter a rescue truck loaded with furniture and accompanied by the men and women of the rescue service, their faces clearly reflecting the horrors of the past few days. The streetlights were still working, as were the window displays of the retail shops, which shone brightly. On a side street, a fisherman, who had returned after the initial evacuation, was trying to shovel a path to the door of his house. Across the street, rescue workers passed furniture out of a window and loaded it onto a truck. When we reached the eastern part of the town, we saw burning houses, ignited by the hot lava masses of the volcano, which loomed in front of us. A police sentry stopped us: We were not allowed to proceed further. We pointed to our equipment and our protective helmets, but to no avail. An order is an order!

Spellbound by the immense volcanic activity, we erected our equipment on top of a black hill. The volcanic fissure, originally 5,000 feet long, had shrunk to about 1,800 feet, and displayed an elongated eruption cone. The volcanic activity was now concentrated on seven openings, which spewed fire and lava several hundred yards into the sky. Huge chunks of rock the size of minivans were thrown over the rim of the crater and tossed downwards in a cascade of sparks. Pieces of lava in ever-new and constantly changing fiery configurations were catapulted from the red, glowing abyss of the crater into the dark sky. A nightmare had become reality—yet it was fascinating in its odd and eerie beauty. The hissing, roaring, stomping and thundering caused the black earth beneath our feet to tremble and shake. We felt very small and insignificant compared to the powers of Mother Nature. It was only late at night that we were able to tear ourselves away from this spectacle. We trudged back to the harbor, totally exhausted but filled with unforgettable experiences. With a lot of luck and the help of a friendly police officer, we were able to find modest accommodations in fisherman's hut.

When morning slowly dawned, it was almost ten o'clock. We made our way to the crater after a frugal breakfast from our emergency rations. During the night, a strong southwest wind had helped great masses of ash on the town. In the eastern part of town, the layer of ash was so high that only the tips of the picket fences were visible. Buried stairways leaned against houses like giant black caskets. Some men were desperately trying to shovel the ash from the flat roofs of houses before they collapsed under the weight of the ash. There was no police sentry at the edge of town today to keep us back, and we were able to get so close to the cone of the volcano that we stood at its base. We worked feverishly, filming, photographing, observing and audio-taping, to take advantage of the favorable winds that blew the ash out to sea. Our nerves were taut; "volcano stress" had gripped us and kept us in its grip for the remaining time we spent on the island.

Suddenly, the wind shifted, first to the south and then to the southeast; a storm was rising, the like of which we had never experienced. We took refuge under the roof of a house which was sticking three feet out of the ash. The sky darkened, and clouds of poisonous gases containing muriatic and sulfuric acids made breathing very difficult. The volcanic projectile became larger and denser. It seemed like a giant colossus was tossing firebombs at us, arrogant humans that we were, trying to pry into his secrets! This was what it must have been like 2,000 years ago in Pompeii. We finally fled from the raging elements, and ran as fast as we could towards the volcano Helgafell, which had been dormant for more than 5,000 years. The "bombs" hit our helmets and the black hail pelted our bodies; only with great effort were we able to shield our valuable equipment. At last, we made it to shelter. We were only able to see the nearest houses, and they were buried by the black ash. All the others had disappeared in the rain of black ash. Screaming and roaring in fury, the volcano tossed tons of lava high above the city of Vestmannaeyjar, which seemed to be drowning in the black cascade.

The reports of each of my experiences were published in a number of German newspapers and scientific magazines; my films from Heimaey were shown several times on German television.

I was very attracted to the Hawaiian Islands, not only because of their beauty, but also because of their volcanic origin and activity. I visited almost all of the islands several times, took part in hiking adventures and diving expeditions, but it was only during my latest visit in 1987 that I was able to experience volcanic activity there. From a helicopter, I surveyed the boiling sea of lava in the eastern fissure zone and traversed for hours the still-warm fields of lava leading up to the new crater of Mount Mauna Ulu. My friend, Hermann Luschner, a very gifted painter and also a volcano enthusiast, painted a realistic picture for me of this volcano at the height of eruption. This painting has a very special place in our living room.

The Bald Eagle
1971–1972

I was watching the eagle through my binoculars as it rose into the air with the mighty strokes of its wings, circling overhead with a majestic calmness. Anyone watching these rare birds intently will understand why the eagle has become the symbol of so many ruling monarchies, and the United States, too. I had been commissioned to design and sculpt a very special model of a large bird and, right away, the majestic eagle was my choice. To create such a delicate work, one has to observe the living bird in its natural habitat. So, I travelled to the eagle sanctuaries, of which there are only very few in Germany. There, I found not only the best conditions for observing the free-flying birds, but also the opportunity to study the correct proportions and other details from a close-up vantage point. During my quest, I also went to the sanctuary of the Rheinfels castle, where I became friendly with the falconer. When I told him of my mission, he supported me in every way possible. I was especially interested in seeing the big bird swoop down on a piece of bait, since this position seemed to be the best one for my purpose: it offered optimal conditions, from a technical and an artistic point of view.

I observed and photographed this sequence of motion very closely, in order to capture all the important details. The falconer was very patient with me, and coaxed the mighty eagle into landing onto his gloved hand time and time again. Several times, I was allowed to let the eagle land on my own arm, since I was by now acquainted with it. This was truly a very special experience, when the large wings darkened the sky above me and the eagle gently landed on my leather-cushioned arm. I used a cane to brace myself in order to provide a stable perch for the heavy bird.

I continued my studies at other eagle sanctuaries and when I returned home after several weeks, I immediately began to sculpt my impressions in clay. I designed an eagle that is landing on its nest with a captured skunk, eagerly awaited by two of its offspring. It was a very extensive model, composed of many, many parts. The creation of the nest, consisting of limbs and twigs, was very complicated. The completed model was accepted by the management, and we could now start making the mother molds, which consisted of more than 30 parts. Substantial props held the wings in place and supported them when the mass of porcelain grew soft during the firing process. We finally had a few examples ready for painting. Once again, it was very important to get as close to the natural colors as humanly possible, and I spent many hours with Guenter Neubauer while he painted the first sample. However, when the first cost calculations were completed, they far exceeded the estimates of our marketing department; I had to redo the model in a less complicated form. At the same time, one of our U.S. importers suggested that I create a bald eagle rather than the golden eagle that I had designed. A bald eagle, the national bird of the United States, would be more readily accepted than the golden eagle. So once again, I went on an expedition to the various sanctuaries to observe the rare bald eagle. I soon discovered that there is really very little difference in the bodies structure of these tow birds. Most obvious was the lack of feathers on the bald eagle's legs and, of course, the completely different color design of the feathers.

Back in my studio, I went to work, simplifying the model to make it more cost-effective. I did away with the nest, the two eaglets and the prey. However, I hardly changed the position of the eagle; I only accentuated the typical features of the bald eagle. I also rearranged the branches underneath the nest, making it appear that it had always been this way. I received the highest praise from our management team for the completed sculpture. It was supposed to be produced in a limited edition of only 200 pieces, and sold only to the most qualified dealers. I then developed a wooden base with a brass plate for engraving, to accentuate this very valuable porcelain sculpture. I felt a great sense of pride when a United States trade commission presented my sculpture to Gerald Ford, at that time the President of the United States.

A Visit From my Father
Summer 1973

We had not seen each other for more than 25 years, but now my father had arrived for a visit from the United States. After my mother's death in New Zealand, he had lived by himself for many years, finally travelling to California to visit my sister Inge. He liked it there so much that he decided to stay. He lived in a small house on my brother-in-law Jim's property and, with his expertise in foreign languages, was able to land a very interesting job as host at the Paul Masson winery. He really enjoyed taking care of his three grandchildren, Victor, Chris and Nanette, when their parents were away.

Now he had returned to Germany, and was awed by the postwar "Economic Miracle" (which really was not a miracle, but the result of long, hard years of reconstruction). When my father left home in 1949, many cities still lay in ruins, and a rapid recovery did not seem possible, even though its foundation had been laid by the introduction of the new German D-Mark.

We walked together through the woods near Coburg and talked about many things. I spoke about my failed first marriage and the happiness of my second one, and about my first professional successes and future prospects. He talked about their new beginning in New Zealand and my mother's early death. Just before she died, she had voiced the opinion that I should seek a divorce. With her motherly instincts, she sensed that my marriage would not work out.

Now my father was living in California, and quite content, but in retrospect saw many things in a different light. We came to the mutual

101

conclusion that it might have been better had they not left Germany at all. He would have had great job opportunities during the reconstruction years. But who could foresee that the war-ravaged, partitioned Germany would develop into such a very prosperous country? Hindsight is always easier than foresight, but it was useless to cry over spilt milk.

This would not be the last visit to his native Germany for my father. Almost 80 years old, he promised to return when his physical condition allowed it, and he made good on that promise. He took walks with my family or we visited towns and cities in the area. We also had a reunion with his two sisters and their families, who lived not too far from Coburg. We all enjoyed these reunions, talking about old times. All of my father's relatives had been expelled by the Poles from Silesia after the war, and had to live under very depressing circumstances for the first few years afterwards. We had had very little contact with them over the years, since, despite his Jewish background, my uncle Eugen had been an avid supporter of Hitler. He died soon after the end of the war, a broken man. My father was never able to forgive him his Nazi beliefs. A few months before my father died at the age of 85, I visited him for the last time in California. He was already terminally ill then, but never let on. I had the impression that he had saved all his remaining strength for my visit, and I think that we both felt that this was the last time we would see each other. He was very proud of me, for he was able to experience the gratitude and appreciation given to me by the many Hummel collectors in the United States.

New York
January 1977

I looked around me, overwhelmed by what I saw. This was New York City, truly a metropolis! Skyscrapers wherever I looked, interspersed by the deep ravines of the streets through which I had walked only a short time before. Now I was standing on top of the Empire State Building in the center of Manhattan. The sun was slowly setting in the West, and in the growing darkness, more and more lights shone in thousands of windows. The long lines of cars seemed like tiny red and white glow worms from my vantage point. No matter where I looked, I could track the trail of streetlights clear up to the horizon.

The first visit to New York City for anyone is likely to be a most overwhelming experience. Even though I had seen many photographs and films about this unique city, the actuality far surpassed anything else. Not even the best movie can replace personal experience. Financial expert Karl-Heinz Mueller and technical expert Erich Pechthold from our top management team were my guides, and shaped my first impressions of the city. This January 1977 was one of the coldest ever on the East Coast. Even the ocean had frozen along the Northeast coastline. I had donned the thick fur coat that had once belonged to Franz Goebel. Wilhelm Goebel presented it to me after his father's sudden death, since I was about the same size as he. (I still wear the coat today.)

During my many trips to the United States, I have visited New York City often, and explored it. Joan Ostroff, a native New Yorker and a close friend of mine, was especially instrumental in showing me the various faces of the city. With her, but often just by myself, I have walked the streets of Manhattan, because that is the best way to become acquainted with a city. I have visited museums, art galleries, theaters, concerts, exhibitions, and, particularly, ballet performances. Often, I just strolled through the streets or sat on the steps of the large public library among all the young people, watching the passersby.

The saying goes, "There is nothing that cannot happen in New York City," and in a sense, this is true. One can find people from all over the world in this giant melting pot, and to an artist especially, this place offers a myriad of new ideas. I am aware that many Americans do not like New York City. The city's dark sides, of which any metropolis has its share, are probably more pronounced here. The media also contributes its share to New York's bad image by reporting the distressing events that happen there in such gory detail. As far as I am concerned, New York City will always have the appeal of a world metropolis, and I visit it whenever I have the chance.

The Biggest Boy
1977–1978

Wilhelm Goebel had summoned me, and now we were sitting with Dieter Schneider in the conference room. The subject was the newly established Goebel Collector's Club. Dieter Schneider had found a suitable building with a beautiful lot in Tarrytown, New York, and it had been purchased by the Goebel company. Wilhelm Goebel proceeded to tell me of his plan: "We have in mind that you should once again create a giant 'Merry Wanderer' figurine for the entrance of the club building, just like the one that stands outside the factory here." The critical look on my face grew even more pronounced as he continued. "This second 'Merry Wanderer' has to be considerably bigger than the first one, because in America, everything is bigger than here." Then Dieter Schneider told me the date when this new facility would be opened with a special ceremony, at which time this giant Hummel figurine would be unveiled. Whereas the creation of the first "super" figurine for the 100th anniversary of the Goebel company had presented numerous problems for me, this second one surely would not be any easier! But after a brief moment of calculation, I accepted this new challenge, and said that I would get it done somehow.

Based on my experiences with the first figurine, I began with the preparations for the new project. The biggest problem was finding a room large enough at ground level. Using my studio was completely out of the question, due to the much larger weight and mostly because of the difficulty in transporting the figurine to the kiln for firing. After a long search, Erich Pechthold offered me a large room in a newly constructed building for the duration of the modeling process. I would need a lot more of the special waterproof material, and ordered it from our mill in the quantity that I had calculated to be sufficient. Then I made a drawing for a turntable in the correct dimension and strength, and had it built by our carpenters and mechanics.

Even though I could fall back on my experiences with the first giant figurine, new problems would crop up with this one, due to its enormous size. I had to fashion special pillars to support individual parts of the figurine and to take care that the clay did not dry out. Every evening before I went home, I had to cover the figurine with a huge sheet of special foil. As the sculpture grew in size, I had to use a ladder to work on it, and often hit my head on the ceiling.

The cutting of the figurine into various parts, and the removal of these parts was especially nerve-wracking. Many strong arms were necessary for this part of the project, and caused a jostling and crowding around the piece. After the first firing, I was in for quite a jolt: On many parts, but especially on the head, large cracks had appeared, many of them almost ½ inch in size. In defiance of my orders, the time allotted for the cooling-off of the figurine had been shorted; thus, the cracks occurred. I had to use a bag full of tricks to fill these cracks with groundup clay and glazing material, and restore the stability of the figurine. But finally, all of the problems were overcome, and the individual parts were soon on their way to the United States. In the meantime, I had a massive foundation built in Tarrytown, the upper layer of which, together with the figurine, could be lifted off— just in case "The Big Boy" needed to be moved at any time.

When I arrived in Tarrytown in April 1978, there awaited an expert assembly team, equipped with all the necessary hoists. Without further ado or problems, we were able to assemble the individual parts. I only had to work the contact areas over in a few places. When completion of the figurine reached its final stage, there were daily traffic jams on the busy street in front of the building. Curious people would slow down or even stop their cars to see what we were doing there. Only extended horn-honking could get them moving again— until the next jam. A cool breeze blew in from the Hudson River and I was grateful for the warm jacket someone had lent me. After completing the last details, I could finally fly to California for a well-deserved vacation. (My story of "The Making of the Big Merry Wanderer" has been published in "Insight"-magazine Vol. 2, No. 2, of the Goebel Collectors

Club. In 1989 the Goebel Collectors Club changed its name to M.I. Hummel Club and moved to Pennington, New Jersey. The Big Boy was still in Tarrytown the following years. In 1994 the giant figurine was transported to Rosemont, Illinois. During my visit there I did some necessary restoration. In 1996 he will stand in front of the new home of the M.I. Hummel Club in Rosemont.)

The Grand Canyon

May 1978

I was sitting all alone atop a steep rock admiring the birthday present that I had given to myself: the Grand Canyon in its entire majestic beauty, a stone-carved witness of a constant geological shift and its results. It was one of the most fabulous landscapes on earth in its breath-taking uniqueness. I had read a lot about the Grand Canyon and seen photos, especially those from my friend Dr. Helmut Worch, but the reality was awesome. On this day, the weather was beautifully clear, and with my binoculars, I could see every detail on the northern rim across from me. Far below, I could view the glistening waters of the Colorado River in several places. A variation in the colors of the rocks, made up of numerous layers, caused by the changing angle of the sunlight, gave the entire landscape an almost animated appearance: Fantastic rock formations, which only moments before had shone brightly in the sunlight, sank into bluish shadows that grew constantly longer as the sun set. Crimson-red formations turned into a coppery hue when the full moon slowly appeared from behind a cliff. I sat there for a long time, spellbound by this natural spectacle, until it became completely dark and I could find my way back to the hotel only with difficulty.

That afternoon, I had flown from Las Vegas, with the last leg of the flight over the Grand Canyon; our small plane was constantly shook by the prevailing turbulences. After checking in at the hotel and calling the visitors' center, I rushed to the rim of the Canyon right away and found a secluded vantage point away from the crowds. I had planned to descend into the Canyon the next day, which meant I had to get up very early. At the visitors' center, I had inquired about the paths leading down into the Canyon and was told that going down into the Canyon and coming back up on the same day was nearly impossible. I followed the Bright Angel Trail to the Indian Garden, and then veered off to the lookout point. I took the same route back to the top and was sure that I could have gone all the way to the bottom and back up in one day; three years later, I hiked with Sieglinde down to the Colorado River and back up in one day without any overexertion.

On a journey down to the bottom of the Canyon, one can experience the great magic of this area when one passes through the four zones of its climate. There may still be snow at the top of the rim, while further down, the cacti are blooming. The well-constructed path leads past various rock formations. Some have a very smooth surface, as if they had been chiseled out by human hands; others show fragile traces of deep erosion. Deep gorges interchange with open areas, and when looking back, one can spot the point of departure far above. At a few watering holes, the traveller has a chance to replenish his water supply—very important for the long trip back. At the bottom, along the Colorado River, which is not too wild at this point, we rested, had something to eat, and gathered strength for the long trip back up. Down at the bottom can be found the "Wishnu Schist," one of the oldest formations in the earth's history. Besides food and water, I brought, of course, my camera, to capture this unusual hike on slides. Even though I have been to the Grand Canyon three times so far, I never get tired of spending hours looking into the huge gorge, and I am always fascinated by its magic beauty.

The Hummel Festival in Eaton

June 1978

The applause reverberated through the open tent for several minutes, reflecting the enthusiasm of the audience when we announced the winners of the M.I. Hummel "Look-Alike" contest. "We"—Joan Ostroff, Alan Hamel and me—acted as the jury. Each of us had a scorecard and a list of all contestants; we judged them by applying specific criteria. To arrive at the winners, we averaged our three sets of scores. It was not always easy to pick the best ones, because all participating children had been diligently costumed and groomed by their parents. While the mothers sewed the clothes and styled the hair, the fathers created the "by-work," such as fences, postaments and trees. The younger children especially often had a difficult time in maintaining the pose and facial expression of the figurine they were representing during the time of presentation.

At the Hummel festival in Eaton, Ohio, organized by Robert Miller, I had a full program. After judging the children, I had to rush over to the main building where a long line of collectors were waiting for me to sign their newly acquired Hummel figurines. Collectors, dealers and onlookers from across the United States had assembled here. Robert Miller displayed his collection of extremely rare figurines, Joan Ostroff held seminars and dealers offered old and new Hummels for sale. It was really a country-fair atmosphere, with people filling the exhibition halls and stalls out in the open at the large fairgrounds.

It was at this festival that I really experienced for the first time the true enthusiasm of collectors for their beloved Hummel figurines, and I was complimented from all sides for the creation of the models. They watched with great interest while I worked on a clay model that I had brought. At the same time, I had to answer many questions from the collectors. A barrage of flashes from cameras exploded in front of me as I rushed to the next building for another program. On the way, I was constantly stopped by collectors, who not only wanted their figurines signed, but also books and catalogs. There was just no place at the fairgrounds where I could hide for a moment's respite or a quick snack. Sometimes I felt overly taxed, but I fulfilled every request. It was only that night on the way back with Joan Ostroff to our hotel in Richmond that I was able to relax a little for the first time that day.

There was very little change in the Festival in the ensuing years, except for some novel events like the "Volksmarch." Rick Dolan, who was the top salesman of our import firm, Ebeling & Reuss, had the great idea of making an RV available to us. Now I had a place to which I could retire for short rests or a quick bite to eat. There I also had the opportunity to give a TV interview to a charming young lady, which was later aired nationwide on "PM Magazine."

I was deeply impressed by the fervor and enthusiasm of the American Hummel collectors, not only at the Eaton Festival, but also at my other promotions across the States. They were interested in knowing every detail about the origin or the production of every Hummel figurine. Their main goal, however, was to meet personally the artist, the man behind their creation, and watch him working on a model. Despite their socioeconomic differences, the collectors belonged to one group with the same interest.

Grand Opening
June 1978

It was a moment filled with tension. Would everything go according to plan in the unveiling of "The Big Boy"? We had rehearsed several times, and it had all gone well. But now, a very large group of guests was assembled in front of the figurine here in Tarrytown, waiting expectantly for the great moment. After a short address. Wilhelm Goebel, Utz Stocke and Dieter Schneider pulled on the rope together. Slowly, the giant figurine appeared from the covering to the thundering applause of the crowd. Guenter Neubauer and I removed the remnants of the covering and then Joan Ostroff joined us. The six of us posed for pictures as cameras clicked and hummed, and the spectators rushed up to us, forming a huge crowd around "The Big Boy."

Handshakes and congratulations were offered to all of us for this successful work. I knew most of the guests from my previous visits, but many visitors had come from Europe to attend this event. Besides our top management, a group of selected co-workers from Goebel had been flown to the U.S. to celebrate with us. Among them were my colleagues Gunter Granget and Gerhard Bochmann. A large tent had been erected, and since the weather was threatening, a walkway had been built to the new club building. The guests streamed inside to see the remodeled interior; everyone voiced approval for a job well done. A lavish spread of food had been provided in the tent and, after the many customary speeches, we remained there for many hours in a happy circle. Most of our conversation, however, centered on the new collectors club and its rapid expansion, since in this short amount of time, it had become the largest such club in the United States. Now the club had its own headquarters with a gallery, movie theater and service facilities. As its symbol, as well as a landmark, the largest Hummel figurine in the world stood in front of the building.

I arose early the next morning and walked the short distance from the Hilton Hotel to the club building. At this early hour, nobody was around, and I could admire the entire layout at my leisure. Dewdrops glistened in the grass and the birds sang. The light of the new day enhanced the warm colors of the figurine. I stood there for a long time, and came to the conclusion that the daring venture to create such a large piece from ceramic had been successful. Completely satisfied, I returned to the hotel and sat down to a good American breakfast.

The Black Grouper
1979

Its big head was now directly in front of me; its large eyes seemed to look at me rather contemptuously. I was able to observe every detail. Its gigantic mouth opened up a little, and I could see the rows of pointed teeth. The slowly pulsating gills reminded me of elephant ears. We stared at each other in this way for some time, until the big fish apparently lost interest in me and swam off, after it decided that I was not its kind of prey. My diving companion, Herb, and I trailed after it at a safe distance, watching it for quite some time while Herb took some pictures with his underwater camera. The other fish around us seemed tiny in comparison with this giant, which floated along majestically while hardly moving its fins. Unfortunately, I had left my own camera behind and so was unable to take my own pictures, pictures that would be the dream of any diver. But this encounter will live on in my memory.

I had come to the Virgin Islands for an educational trip, and stayed at a resort that had a large diving center. I intended to study coral fish for future models, since the first models that I had made had been very well received. I had given one of my porcelain fish to the director of the diving center. He was so delighted with it that he let me dive in very special areas with Herb, his diving instructor.

On this particular day, Herb and I ventured far out to sea. He knew the whereabouts of an old wreck of a mail steamer, which had gone down in the 19th century, that was rarely explored, due to its great distance from shore. It took a long time before he located the wreck and we could throw down the anchor. Then we dove down to the sea floor, about 100 feet below us, and it was not too long before we spotted the dark hull of the ship, which seemed to be resting on its side. The hull still appeared to be in fairly good shape, and we entered it through an open hatch. The interior was just teeming with fish of all kinds. Everything inside the wreck was covered with coral and sponges, which formed a habitat for the reef-dwelling creatures. The wreck, resting on a sandy bottom, seemed like a world unto itself, but one could only guess at the multicolored magnitude of life at this depth. Only with the aid of searchlights or flashlights can the actual multitude of colors in the bluish depth be seen.

Besides butterfly fish the size of a hand, several large groupers stuck their heads out through openings, and a green moraine showed its sharp teeth. A large blue angelfish floated by, while a green parrot-fish nibbled on the coral. The long tentacles of a lobster protruded from a dark crevice and were moving slowly in the water. Both of us were simply awed by the magic of this underwater world, and pointed out new sights to each other. At one place, the ship's hull was torn open, and we could see out into the open water through the ship's ribs. It was here that we encountered the giant grouper.

After we rose to the surface again and climbed into our boat, we were still under the spell of this fantastic underwater adventure. Herb, who was a skilled diving instructor, had been familiar with these waters for ten years, but had not been to this particular wreck in a long time. He told me, "I have never seen a grouper like him," adding "This one is the king of the wreck. He must have weighed better than 800 pounds." During the long voyage back to the diving center, our conversation kept returning to this giant of the sea.

The True Story
Fall 1979

I was commissioned to design a completely new nativity scene, based entirely on my own concepts. With this order from the Goebel management team in front of me, I was trying to visualize how this new crib set should look. Almost every nativity set I had ever seen treated the birth of Jesus as a fairy tale, with crowned kings and colorful shepherds. The M.I. Hummel nativity sets in various sizes, and the other sets developed by the Goebel team, were no exceptions. Over the years, I had visited many nativity displays in different European countries; all of them, often done in luxurious splendor, contained figurines clad in colorful garments from every conceivable era. Modern figures were frequently designed as abstracts. I could not find a single crib set in the reference books that looked the way it should have 2,000 years ago.

Even the most ardent skeptic cannot argue that the birth of Christ occurred, a fact documented by witnesses and scriptures. For centuries, the event has been embellished, for whatever reasons. I began to study books and reports about His birth by historians. I was determined to create a nativity that would reflect, as closely as possible, the actual era. I studied the clothing styles that were worn by the Palestinian people at that time; I also tried to find out if the animals then resembled the ones that we see today.

When everything was finalized in my mind, I started to sculpt the clay models, working in a size that was between the small and large M.I. Hummel nativity sets. By using this inbetween size, the individual

This is the first clay model of an eagle and two baby birds in a nest, which I sculpted in 1971. (Photo courtesy of Goebel)

I made this clay model of a dancing girl in 1971.

In June 1944 I sculpted this bust of my sister Ingeborg, in the studio of
Professor Poertzel in Coburg.

In 1958 I had the privilege of sculpting the singing star Bibi Jones
in a film studio in Berlin.

In 1958 I created a large aluminum sculpture entitled Icedance. I worked on it in the locksmith workshop of the W. Goebel factory in Roedental, during a factory vacation.

In 1988 I demonstrated my sculpting techniques in Tarrytown, New York. (Photo courtesy of Beverly J. Spadaro)

In 1980 I destroyed the resin model for the Goebel Collector's Club figurine. (Photo courtesy of Goebel)

I always enjoy demonstrating sculpting on the promotional tours. This one took place in 1983.

I sculpted this bust of my daughter Suzanne in 1951.

This nude was created in 1960.

I greatly enjoyed creating the Falcon in 1961. (Photo courtesy of Goebel)

This clay model for a bust of Sister Maria Innocentia Hummel was sculpted in 1964. (Photo courtesy of Goebel)

A few days after his death in 1969, I sculpted this bust of Franz Goebel.

My two sons, Stephan and Martin, are the subjects of this 1977 double bust.

I was able to indulge my love of underwater sea life when I created these coral fish for Goebel in 1978. (Photo courtesy of Goebel)

In 1979 I researched and sculpted this historical nativity set for Goebel, which has proven to be one of the most popular. (Photo courtesy of Goebel)

I created this dancing couple in 1982.

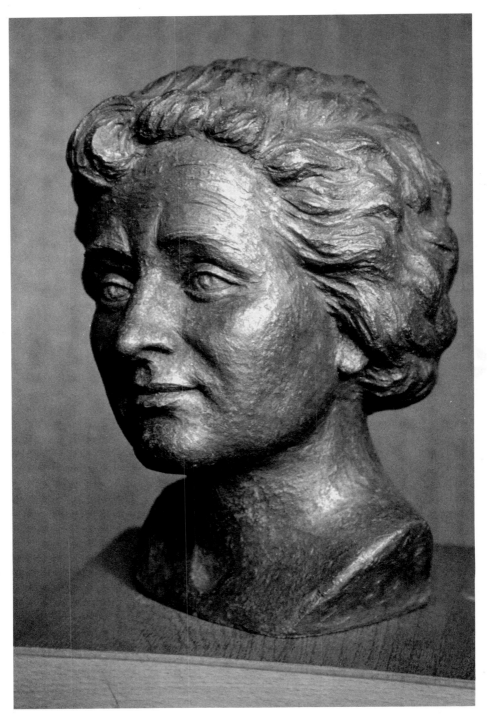

In 1990 I sculpted my beloved "better half," Sieglinde.

figurines would be large enough to show off all the necessary details without raising the cost of the finished product. I did not design kings with crowns; instead, I portrayed them as distinguished gentlemen who had arrived at the nativity by horse, camel and elephant. As a symbol of the future, I arranged the straw on which the Christ Child lay in the shape of a cross. My only reference to a supernatural being was a small kneeling angel raising its hand in a blessing. All of the figurines' details were executed in a realistic manner, and I stuck to a rig authenticity in the painting. So, I created a nativity with figurines that are unique and yet show the birth of Christ as it could have happened. The best compliment (and also an endorsement of my concepts of authenticity) was that this particular set, the "Historic Christmas Nativity Crib Set," was frequently purchased by churches.

A Work Day in June
June 1980

As was my usual routine every morning, I enjoyed the water cascading over my skin, and did my exercises under the shower–they relieved the back spasms that I had suffered for years. To improve my mobility, I had invented some of these exercises myself, and I performed them daily. After a final cold shower à la Kneipp (a 19th-century German physical therapist), I really felt fit. I always took the time for a leisurely breakfast, even if it meant getting up earlier. While listening to classical music, Sieglinde and I sat in our rustic breakfast nook, enjoying the meal. After a quick glance at the morning paper, I took off and drove the four miles to the factory. Occasionally, I would ride my bike to work when the weather was nice. But then, I wouldn't follow the street, but took a small path winding through pastures and woods, accompanied by the singing of the birds. Their chirping always put me in a good mood for the daily chores ahead. Whenever I had to supervise an apprentice, my first concern was for him, and I discussed the work planned for the day with him thoroughly. Then I walked over to the place where my assistant, Helmut Eber, was assembling a figurine from its individual mold parts. It was always important in this work that during the assembly the position of the figurine not change in the least.

   Looking at my appointment book, I noticed that there was a conference about quality control scheduled in a short time, so I did not have a chance inbetween times to work on one of my models, which had been sitting overnight in a "wet" cabinet. Instead, I went into my "office" (a fold-out desk), and started working on papers that had accumulated during the past few weeks. I had to fill out form papers, requisition model cards and register all the new Hummel models in the company model log. The half hour passed quickly and I hurried to the conference room. The quality-control sessions, which had been held for several months, proved to be very effective. A number of figurines were selected at random right from the kiln and spread out on the conference table. Seated around the large table were members from every branch of the production department, and they judged each piece individually according to a very specific point system. We kept minutes of these meetings, and all problems, as well as peculiarities of certain figurines, were discussed with the supervisory personnel.

Back at my studio, I finally was able to begin work with a clay model that was almost finished, but I was constantly interrupted by phone calls. Then, the head of the casting department called to say that he had a problem getting a figurine's head out of its master mold Armed with my special tools, I rushed over to his workroom and worked on the mold until the problem was solved. When I returned to my studio, another casting-department supervisor was waiting for me to show me a figurine's leg with a flaw in it. A crease on the shoe went only as far as the casting seam. I made a note to check the work-model for this particular piece and, if necessary, to have it retouched. I had not done very much on the new model when the bell sounded for lunch. Everybody in the factory hurried somewhere: some to our large dining room, others went home for a rushed meal, and a few stayed at their workplaces and "brown-bagged" it. Sieglinde had packed a lunch for me, so I ate it before I started on my usual lunchtime stroll. With my car or bike, I rode to the nearby woods, and walked up the hill with quick strides. I already spotted the wild strawberries from a distance, growing on a sunny slope. At this time of the year, I always carried a small container with me and filled it with these little, fragrant berries. I ate a few as a well-deserved dessert. While picking them, I could already savor the delicious punch in which we would use them. Then I looked at my watch. It was time to rush back to my studio if I didn't want to be late! I grabbed a few of the finest berries—it seems as if the best ones are never found until last—tossed them into my container and hurried back to the car.

I was able to spend the afternoon putting the final touches on the work-model without too many interruptions. Afterwards, I prepared another work-model from an original Hummel drawing that I had picked up at the Goebel archives. The proper creation of a clay model is of the greatest importance to the final figurine. You should only start on such a project if you are really in a creative mood. You have to have the image of the new figurine in your head already. If it is a pleasing motif, and you are creatively inclined, this combination will almost always result in a very attractive, successful figurine.

Suddenly, I realized that I had not eaten since noon and I was hungry. I viewed my clay model from all sides and felt very pleased with my creation. In my mind, I could already see the finished figurine, and found it to my liking. So, I covered the model with a plastic bag and put it away for the night in the "wet" cabinet. (Without the plastic wrapping around the model, the moisture tends to rise to the surface and in the process, dissolves the chalk or lime contained in the clay, leaving white chalk particles on the surface that are almost impossible to remove later on.) Nightfall was approaching when I got into my car and drove home after a long day's work.

Hawaii

May 1981

From here, it was an overwhelming sight. We looked down on a valley that was rimmed by ragged cliffs and overgrown with tropical greenery. Far below was a small stretch of beach and the dark-blue waters with their pounding waves. A white cloud formation above us accentuated the contrast of colors. I had come here with Sieglinde, to Kauai, during our trip to Hawaii. Now we were standing at the Kalalau lookout point, admiring this beautiful panorama. Colibris were darting by in their search for nectar, and the soft breezes soothed our skin. Suddenly, we were shaken from our dreamworld by a man close to us, who began to dance around, jumping from one leg to the other, shouting jubilantly. When he calmed down a little, we asked him the reason for his joyous eruption. "This is the sixth time that I have visited Kauai," he explained, "and every time, it rained and the sky was darkened by threatening clouds. This is the first time that I have a clear view, and I think that is enough of a reason for my excitement. How often have you been here?" He could hardly believe that we were so lucky on our very first visit to have gorgeous weather. We then strolled along the ridge and looked down into the Waimea Canyon, planning to walk through it for a little way. Here we were not too far from the rainiest place on earth, and it made us appreciate the clear blue sky even more.

Our first journey together had led us to this beautiful archipelago in the middle of the Pacific Ocean, and we visited four islands there, each of which has its own particular landscape. In Honolulu, I had a

121

strange encounter at the famous Waikiki Beach. While Sieglinde went shopping, I rented a Hobie catamaran and sailed out into the ocean. With a stiff breeze helping me, I made good speed after getting through the surf close to the beach. Suddenly, I was no longer alone—six dolphins surrounded me and, without any effort, kept pace with my boat. One of them even swam between the two hulls of the cat and let me touch it. At one point, it raised its head out of the water and seemed to smile at me. These aquatic mammals accompanied me for quite some time, until they got bored and veered off.

By that time, I also thought I had ventured out far enough, so I turned around and headed back to shore to get my diving gear. With equipment on board, I set sail again towards the spot where I had been, hoping to find the dolphins again. Even though I snorkeled more than half a mile from the boat, I couldn't find them, and headed back to the cat, disappointed. And suddenly, they were there again, circling the catamaran! Again, one came very close to me in the water. He was apparently the bravest of the bunch, and most likely the same one that I had stroked before. This game went on for quite a while, though I was a rather clumsy playmate who quite often had to surface for air. Then, as suddenly as they appeared, they disappeared into the vast blue depths of the ocean. I had frequently watched trained dolphins and had studied them thoroughly before I sculpted one. This episode with dolphins in their own habitat, however, was a lot more exciting for me.

I had undertaken long trips with Sieglinde in the Volcano National Park on the big island, and showed her the fantastic lava fields. We were both very impressed by the kaleidoscope of colors on the surface of these fields. Unfortunately, there was no volcanic activity on the east rift at this time. A special attraction for us was the Kona-Surf Hotel, which is situated high up in the lava cliffs. After nightfall, the ocean was illuminated by strong searchlights from the hotel terrace. The lights attracted a large mass of small crustaceans, which in turn attracted a number of giant manta rays taking in their dinners with wide-open fangs.

On Maui, we stayed at the Sheraton, which I knew from my first visit to the island. Adjacent to the hotel is a huge cliff that juts out into the ocean and from which every evening a native jumped into the sea after he had set fire to a row of torchlights. Below this cliff was a reef where we went scuba diving. The coral reef, only a few feet beneath the surface, astounded us with its beautiful array of colors. The next day, we ascended Haleakala, where we walked for many miles through the fantastic volcanic landscape of the vast Caldera, until the threatening clouds forced us to retreat.

The exciting days in Hawaii passed all too quickly. Sieglinde took a flight back to good old Germany, while I flew to the mainland United States to start a promotional tour. Hawaii seems to hold a very special attraction for me, and I am sure that I will visit it again.

Cousin Sonja
June 1981

I recognized her voice immediately when she called me in my Des Moines, Iowa, hotel room. She apologized that she had almost completely forgotten German, since she had spoken English for the past 42 years. We agreed to meet at the hotel, and I eagerly looked forward to this reunion.

I had last seen Sonja in 1939, when she emigrated with her parents from Nazi Germany to New Zealand. At 14 years old, she had been a beautiful but shy girl, who looked to her future in an unknown land with a little apprehension. My Aunt Annemarie, one of my mother's sisters, had adopted her, since she could not have children of her own. During the war, of course, we had no contact whatsoever with each other. It was only a number of years after the war that we learned through my Aunt Grete, my mother's other sister, that Sonja was married and living in the United States. Later one, my father sent me a photograph of her, which had been taken during her visit with my sister. So, I recognized her right away as she stood before me, vivacious, pretty, and with that familiar voice. She had read in the newspaper that I would be appearing in Des Moines for a promotion. Sonja called the shop right away and told them that she was a relative of mine. They apparently didn't quite believe her and tried to brush her aside. But finally, she was able to find out the address of my hotel, and there she was! We had a lot to talk about: our lives and experiences during the past 42 years. It was very late when she said goodbye and drove home. But I could not go to sleep. On the same floor as my room, there was a party going on. Most of the rooms were open and there were people everywhere, drinking and talking. The volume of the hubbub grew, of course, with the rate of alcohol consumption—there was no way I could fall asleep with all that noise. But I needed to, because the promotion on the following day would be very strenuous. We expected a lot of visitors, and I was to present the governor of the state of Iowa with a bald eagle figurine. So I finally asked the celebrants to be a little less noisy. But they laughed at me and instead, invited me to join them. But I certainly couldn't do that. It would be impossible to do a promotion with a hangover! Finally, I plugged my ears with cotton and dozed off around dawn, when the party out in the hallway was over.

The next day, I was much too busy to feel tired. The store was overflowing with collectors who wanted my signature on figurines that they had just purchased. Sonja had also come, and assisted me. Later, at dinner, she confided to me that she never thought for a minute that such enthusiasm for Hummel figurines and their creator existed.

Thereafter, every time I had a scheduled promotion in Des Moines, I planned for a few open days in my itinerary, so that I could see Sonja. She showed me the city and the surrounding area; I stayed with her and her husband and enjoyed the atmosphere of a cozy home after many nights in a hotel. The last letter that I received from Sonja sounded like a final goodbye. She had become very ill; soon after, I learned that she had passed away.

The TV Show
June 1981

Our Canadian business associates had arranged everything perfectly; I was to take an excursion by boat on this particular Sunday to see the bays and islands around Vancouver, accompanied by two pretty ladies from management. I had looked forward to seeing these sights for some time. But, nothing came of it! Quite suddenly, our plans went up in smoke—I received a phone call from Cleveland, Ohio. I was scheduled to be a guest on the well-known Dave Patterson show televised there. With a heavy heart, I canceled the boat trip and drove to the airport early in the morning to catch the first plane for Cleveland. There I was, aloft in the plane, sadly looking down from the window on this interesting array of islands, which I could only see from a bird's-eye perspective.

Rick Dolan, our representative, was already waiting for me at the Cleveland airport and drove me straight to the television studio. We had an informative chat with the assistant producer of the show; I was then introduced to Dave Patterson. We hit it off beautifully. I asked him shortly before air-time to speak slowly and distinctly, since my English was far from perfect. Suddenly, it grew quiet in the large auditorium, a voice said, "Stand by" and started counting backwards, as if it were a rocket launching. I could see a look of stage fright on the faces of my companions, Rick and Mike, even though they were just standing in the wings. However, I was very calm in the glare of the lights. After all, what could happen to me? It was a strange feeling, though, to know that beyond the lenses of the cameras were probably several million viewers, all observing me with critical eyes.

The studio audience was arranged in tiered rows of seats. Dave asked his questions clearly and I had no problem understanding him; only once did I ask him to repeat a question. (At subsequent interviews across the United States, I found that this experience was not always to be repeated. Some interviewers asked their questions using a lot of slang and, since time was short, they also spoke very rapidly; I had a very hard time understanding them.) This first show went very well, and I fielded all questions, even those from the audience, without much effort.

The half-hour show was over faster than I had expected. and after a round of applause from the audience, the last red camera light went off. (Dave Patterson apparently was very pleased with my performance, because he immediately asked me to come back to his show when I next visited Cleveland. I did just that, two years later. In the meantime I had gained a lot of experience and was much more professional the next time around in front of the cameras.)

Rick and Mike had watched me from the wings and were evidently relieved that the interview had gone so well. Naturally, that was cause for celebration, so we all met at a seafood restaurant that evening. Here, far from the ocean's shore, we were served one of the finest seafood platters I have ever eaten.

The next day, when I arrived at the gallery, which was located in a large mall, I could see from a distance that a large crowd had gathered. I was showered with applause as I took my seat at an elevated table to sign M.I. Hummel figurines that were handed to me by the enthusiastic collectors. This went on for two days, interrupted only by short sculpting demonstrations. I took great care to answer each collector's question with patience and diligence. Many of them shook my hand, which was numb from all the signing, or expressed their admiration for my work. On the morning of the second day, Rick, with whom I had been staying, brought many boxes of figurines out into his garden, where I sat signing them, accompanied by the chirping of the song birds.

A Family Vacation

August 1982

Helpful neighbors came from all sides to assist us in the maneuvering of our camper into the proper position. We had waited for two days until this spot, one of the most beautiful camping sites on the Adriatic Sea in Yugoslavia, became available. As soon as the previous occupant had vacated the premises, I pulled up with our trailer; we now had this ideal camping spot for three weeks. We were situated on a small, hilly peninsula studded with old trees, overlooking the Adriatic on which our little boat was riding the waves, tethered to a buoy.

The entire family pitched in to erect the big tent and secure it with ropes. In previous years we had experienced strong storms on this beautiful coast—many a tent that had not been secured properly had been blown away or shredded by the gales. By the time the sun sank in a crimson-red ball, we had completed our task. Now our vacation could really begin; we had looked forward to it for a long time. There would be no cooking at home tonight! Instead, we went to a restaurant located on an old, romantic estate. There, at a large table, we sat with friends and enjoyed a delicious seafood platter, washed down with a delectable local wine. (The children, of course, had to make do with Coke.) My friend Heinz had brought his sailboat, too, and the two of us planned to explore the nearby uninhabited islets, which lay off the ragged coast. We sat together under the star-bright sky for a long time, sipping the delicious wine while a slight sea-breeze made us forget the heat of the day. The five boys, my two and Heinz' three, soon tired and went to sleep.

The next morning, we all joined forces to make a big breakfast. While Stephan and Martin set the table, their mother made coffee and boiled eggs; I filmed the whole event with my camera. An hour later we were on our way to a rocky island that was located far out to sea. Since the wind was not favorable, I started the boat's small engine and we headed straight for our destination. Martin lay on a surfboard behind us, which we towed with a long line. Everyone was a little bit excited, since it seemed like a big adventure to be heading for parts unknown. As our sailboat rounded the island, we discovered a beautiful bay where we dropped anchor and went ashore to explore the island. Small paths led inland, and large green lizards, which were sunning themselves there, fled before our approaching steps. Seagulls flew above us, screeching with their shrill voices. Flowers were not plentiful on this scraggy island, but each one had attracted insects of all kinds. From the highest point of "our" island we had a great panoramic view of Istria's green coast.

Everyone returned to the beach for some underwater exploration. Each one donned underwater gear, and we snorkeled through the crystal-clear sea. When one person would discover something of interest, he would show his discovery to the others.

After a quick lunch, it was each to his own. While Sieglinde read on shore, Stephan and I sailed several miles out to sea. Martin decided to go surfing. The wind began to stir up the seas, and the waves became big. We decided it would be best to return to shore. The sailboat's small motor was hardly a match for the heavy sea and we hardly made any headway, especially since we were towing the surfboard. The wind had shifted and was intensifying. Each time the boat dipped into the valley of a wave, a gush of water soaked the children, who were sitting in the bow. Fortunately, the water ran off through the portholes. The raging sea demanded everyone's total attention, but finally we approached the shore by our campsite. I had to apply all my navigational skills to get through the breakers; one has to transverse the high breakers at the correct angle or the boat will capsize. Martin jumped into the water and dragged the surfboard ashore. Soon, we brought the boat on the beach with a roller. With the sailboat secured tied up, we were glad to have solid ground under our feet again because now the storm was at its height. A severe thunderstorm with lightning unloaded its fury upon us, and the rain poured down in buckets. As rapidly as the storm had developed, it quickly moved on and we again basked in bright sunlight. Martin devoted his time to his "house pet," a giant four-inch Praying Mantis, which he fed with insects as it sat on his shoulders.

Each day of our vacation brought new excitement—nobody got bored. The day of departure arrived all too quickly; all of our gear had to be stowed properly. Using the roller, we raised the boat up onto the roof of our car and stowed the surfboard and tent in the camper. We started home for Coburg early in the morning. Later that year, when winter had settled in, we watched the movies and slides I had taken of this vacation and happily relived those wonderful memories.

Building a Factory
January 1983

The heat was so intense, I feared for my camera. I could only get close enough for a few moments at a time to snap a picture, and then I had to jump back because of the great heat. I wasn't at the site of a glowing lava stream this time, but in the walkway below the tunnel kiln. From there I shot pictures of figurines at their maximum firing temperature. Kilnmaster Oursin had pushed the oven carts apart with a long iron rod so that I could photograph from the walkway one of the carts and its load at the hottest firing zone. Once I had taken a series of shots and was certain that at least some of them would turn out all right, the gap between the carts was closed again. I went straight down to the canteen and downed a cool beer in one big gulp; it felt like even the beer was hissing. Now I understood why the kiln personnel had to drink so much. These pictures were not taken under as difficult conditions as were my photos of volcanic eruptions, but I wanted to create a model of a firing kiln that looked authentic.

Joan Ostroff had an idea: to develop a small factory, or "facsimile" factory as it was later called. Experts, using the facilities of this factory, would show the public the amount of traditional handwork it takes to create their beloved M.I. Hummel figurines. I was asked to assist in this project. The most important steps in our production—modeling, moldmaking, casting and hand painting—were to be shown as realistically as possible. Most of the interior furnishings, such as work desks, tools and material, could be used in their original sizes

131

and forms. Some of the tables had to be made a little smaller due to the lack of space in the facsimile factory.

A decisive factor in the manufacture of porcelain is the extremely high firing temperature of the items. Only through the firing process and the subsequent molecular changes can the fragile casting material be transformed into the rock-hard porcelain. High-grade porcelain, which is created through this costly process, differs considerably from that produced by the cold-cast process. Therefore, I was of the opinion that a kiln was an absolute necessity for our facsimile factory. Using a real kiln was completely out of the question because of its weight; the only possibility open to us was the creation of a correctly sized model from lightweight material. However, an essential part of an oven or kiln is the fiery glow within, and that had to be visible to the factory's visitors. So, the oven itself, with the exception of the original cart with its firewalls, was just a facade. I thought that perhaps one of my slides of the actual oven in Roedental might be enlarged to fit the kiln; when illuminated from behind, it would look like the real thing.

When the facsimile factory was finished, we assembled it again for a final inspection before shipment. The oven was also tested, and we noticed that the "glowing" figurines in it appeared very real. Later, during our United States promotions, I watched, amused, how collectors cautiously approached this imitation "heat." The facsimile factory was set up at numerous locations across the United States and always drew a lot of attention. But unfortunately, we soon discovered that the transport, the needed space, and the breaking down and setting up of the factory, along with the travel expenses of our factory experts was just prohibitively expensive. At first, the travel schedule of the facsimile factory was drastically reduced; finally, it was just terminated. It really is a shame that such an educational project had to be canceled because of the high costs associated with it.

South Bend
July 1983

They all knew me and most of them greeted me enthusiastically as I walked from one exhibit to another, surveying the collectibles on display in the great hall at South Bend, Indiana. I had always wanted to meet the American artists in person, those about whom I had read mostly in newspapers or trade magazines. Many artists had limited themselves to putting their work on collector plates, and the convention in South Bend at this time was primarily a collector-plate show. A number of the artists, though, had their two-dimensional art transposed into figurines by colleagues who were experts in three-dimensional work. Most of these figurines were produced in the Far East, and were of a more or less good quality. Some artists did model their own figurines without the help of previously painted designs. There were a lot of women painters, some who were already famous and some who hoped to be. As one of the few non-American artists attending South Bend, I found the contact and the discussions with my colleagues from the United States very interesting, affording me the opportunity to study in depth my counterparts from that huge melting pot known as the United States of America. European art trends prevailed but had developed over several generations of artists into an independent, American expression of art. Artistic expression ran the gamut, from the super-realistic to the somewhat impressionistic to the highly stylized. Three-dimensional art converted from the two-dimensional contained mostly realistic expressions, often sprinkled with romantic or even comic elements. Comparing figurines based on the works of American

133

artists with our own M.I. Hummel figurines was quite a revelation to me in South Bend.

Artists are individualists; this was most evident at the "artists' breakfast" held the following morning at a beautiful old mansion. Whether it was through their clothing or their mannerisms, each artist expressed his or her unique personality. Even though this event was for artists only, most of them played their roles as if the public were also present. Nobody can jump over his own shadow, and I am no exception.

During the South Bend show, I presented my sculpting demonstration several times a day to a very interested audience. Joan Ostroff provided the commentary about my work or answered questions; I only interjected occasionally. At that time, I was just beginning to develop my demonstration. Now, when I mold a plastiline figurine with my hands, I comment on what I am doing or field questions nonchalantly. I had started doing this kind of display during my appearances on television, where a lot must be shown and explained within a matter of a few minutes. But it's all a part of a rigid training and preparation.

Joan and I were interviewed in South Bend again by the local TV station. The focus of our second evening at the show was the National Association of Limited Edition Dealers (NALED) awards. And I was given an award. Such an honor is, for an artist, not only a confirmation of the appeal and quality of his or her work, but also a challenge for the future. My work has reaped many NALED awards over the years.

On the last evening of the South Bend show, a large group of collectors, retailers and artists attended a banquet in the large hall of the University of Notre Dame. As an award winner, I, with Joan, sat at the head table with the other winners, and our days at South Bend came to a very impressive end.

Meeting the President
January 1984

We stood facing each other, chatting casually. Around us stood officials and VIPs of the German hiking clubs, listening to every word
that was said. Professor Carl Carstens, president of the Federal German Republic, was explaining to me why he had chosen my design
over those of other artists for the Eichendorf plaque, which would
be given to the oldest, most deserving hiking clubs. The President
inquired with great interest about the details in the design and the
technical problems in its manufacture. He seemed really pleased
when I told him that my wife and I hiked regularly. Carstens himself
was an enthusiastic hiker and promoted this healthy exercise whenever he could. For that reason, he was the sponsor of the prestigious
plaque. Cameras clicked away as he expressed his admiration and
appreciation for my work. Then his entourage urged him to move
on, so that he would stay on schedule.

This had all started several months previously, when the Goebel
Porzellanfabrik received a call from the office of the President. He
had decided to sponsor the awarding of a special plaque to outstanding hiking clubs, and his office was looking for a porcelain factory
that would be able to design and manufacture such a thing. As is so
often the case in situations like this, time was of the extreme essence,
since the date for the awarding of the plaque had already been set.
So, I was commissioned to design the award quickly. It was to feature
a portrait of the famous German poet and hiking enthusiast *Freiherr*
(Baron) von Eichendorf on the front and the federal eagle on the

back. The text for the plaque had already been chosen, too, and contained, to my great satisfaction, a word about the need for environmental protection. I went to work immediately.

The plaque was to be five inches in diameter, so I prepared a slightly larger disc of plaster of Paris, taking the shrinkage into account, and modeled the portrait of the poet as a flat relief on it. I determined that, as with a coin, the portrait had to stand out against the white of the porcelain. I made a detailed drawing of the reverse side with the federal eagle and the text and, due to the short time allotted, handed the project over to my assistant, Helmut Eber, for completion.

After management approved the model, we prepared the mother mold in a great hurry, smoothing all the details. Soon we had the first sample ready for a presentation at the President's office. Of course, other ideas and samples from other artists and companies had also been submitted, as the President informed me during our conversation. But his decision to accept mine was almost spontaneous, and we could begin production immediately. Those of us at the company knew that this would not be a large order, but it would be well worth the prestige awarded to Goebel and to me.

I then received an invitation from the President's office to attend the first award ceremony, to be held in Augsburg. Before the official ceremony, which was held in a large auditorium where delegations from all the German hiking clubs assembled with their flags, there was a small reception for a gathering of honored guests. It was here that I had the aforementioned conversation with Carstens. For me, this was the reward for a project well done, and personal recognition as an artist.

The Golden Anniversary

1985

It was hard to believe that the M.I. Hummel figurines were now almost 50 years old, and yet they looked as youthful as ever; their appearance had hardly changed since their debut, when they won the hearts of collectors. In the meanwhile, the Hummel figurines had marched their way into all corners of the earth, and were assured a place in the collectibles market, especially in the United States. I was not there at the very beginning, but had contributed my share during the past 30 years. When I modeled my first M.I. Hummel figurine in 1954, they were only about 20 years old and were just beginning to attract the American collector. There is no rational explanation for the legendary and phenomenal success, over such a long timespan, of these loveable sculptures.

Now their 50th anniversary was approaching, and it was truly a reason to celebrate. I had given a lot of thought as to which figurine would best symbolize this festive occasion. For Sister Hummel's 75th birthday celebration, I had picked a boy and girl with large bouquets of flowers from her artistic legacy, and combined them into one figurine. However, at our meeting at the Siessen Convent, we had agreed upon the Madonna "Supreme Protection" for the birthday figurine, since the convent preferred a religious piece for this particular celebration. But these two children offering bouquets of congratulations symbolized the "Jubileum" or Jubilee of Hummel figurines, so I changed the engraved "75" to a "50." But there was more to come: A very special book, *The Golden Anniversary Book,* containing many

brightly colored pictures, valuable information and background stories, was to be printed. This book was the result of teamwork by Eric
Ehrman and Robert Miller with the photographer, Walter Pfeiffer.
Ehrman conducted a number of informative interviews with me and
many former employees from the 1930s, writing very authentic stories. Personally, I derived great enjoyment from working with Walter
Pfeiffer, and learned to appreciate his ability and knowledge even
more. I advised him on technical problems and also could help him
in photographic matters. The time until the anniversary year passed
quickly with the many preparations and additional work that had to
be done, but brought a welcome break in routine for all of us.

Joan Ostroff thought of a very special surprise; she proposed a
display contest between the dealers of North America (the United
States and Canada were divided into six regions). Only a few weeks
before departing on one of my U.S. promotional tours, Joan informed
me via letter that I was to be the major prize! (Not my person, of
course, but the winners would receive a promotion with me.)

This promotional tour throughout the entire United States was
one of the toughest, most stressful that I ever undertook. The winners of the display contest had not been determined by the time the
tour was scheduled, and my itinerary was set and could not be changed.
As a result, I had to cross the continent several times, from east to
west and from north to south, within the five-week tour. On the other
hand, it turned out to be one of the most successful promotional tours
in the United States.

The Hummel Club Tour

June 1985

The festive mood was peaking; almost everyone danced the "Chicken Dance." That was followed by a polonaise, and a long line of revelers snaked its way between the tables, out the door and around the cars in the parking lot. At times, the chain of dancers broke, but the gap was quickly closed by others. Our accordionist followed us outside into the courtyard and just kept playing. After a few rounds, we danced back inside the garage that was decorated like a hay loft, and plunked down on our seats, exhausted. Our thirst was great on this evening at the hotel Goldene Traube in Coburg, and we quenched it with wine from Franconia and the smooth beer of Coburg (interspersed with a cola or mineral water for those with an even greater thirst). What caused such merriment that lasted late into the night? The "Franconian Evening," the highlight of a good time had by all the globe-trotting Hummel collectors during the Club trips to Europe.

With Sieglinde, my "better half" (I like this expression!), I had been chosen to chaperone a group of collectors during their three-day stay in Coburg. After their arrival the previous night, I had welcomed them on behalf of the Goebel management, and we all enjoyed a wonderful dinner. Sheila, the tour guide from Tallyho Travel, who was sitting at our table, whispered to me that this group was especially nice. They had spent delightful, merry evenings together (especially along the Rhine, of course). Due to the long bus ride, most of the travelers were tired and soon went to their rooms. This suited me just fine because I knew they all would be well rested for the big Franconian Evening the following night.

139

The next morning, I went to the factory very early; the mold
maker, Bluemig, was eagerly awaiting me with an urgent problem—
a mother mold had to be reworked. It seemed that the arm and leg
of a new Hummel figurine could be lifted from the mold only with
extreme difficulty. I finished with this painstaking reworking just in
time to greet our guests in the Information Center, where the tour
guides and interpreters, experts in our technical management and
multilingual secretaries, were waiting for me and the collectors.

The large travel group was to be split up into several smaller
groups that were guided through the factory, each going a separate
way. Because the passageways were narrow in the casting department
and especially in the painting department, overcrowding might have
resulted in the breakage of a valuable figurine, as past experience
had taught us. It was also the reason that we permitted only members of the Hummel Club to tour the factory; all other visitors were
restricted to the special demonstration areas.

In a very short time, the bus had arrived and our guests flocked
into the factory, where I met them at the "birthplace" of the Hummel
figurines and introduced the tour guides and interpreters. While the
collectors were touring the factory, for most of them a highlight of
their trip, I returned to the casting department to make sure that the
reworked mold was functioning properly. I examined the last casting from the adjusted molds, making minor corrections along the
seams. On the way to my studio, I picked up model specifications and
protocol papers at the technical department and discussed a few problems with my coworkers. Then it was time to return to the collectors
because the tour was almost over. I brought several modeling tools
and some clay with me to the projection room. There I moved the
heavy modeling block to the center of the room so that everyone
would be able to see it. I had just turned on the spotlights when I
heard the first guests coming down the hall. Some of them were ani-
matedly discussing the tour, while others were silent, in awe of what
they had seen. It took a while before everyone had arrived and were
seated.

Then I began, using only my hands, to model a figurine from
the lump of clay; it was not very long before the visitors, watching
attentively, could recognize the "Merry Wanderer." Normally, I couldn't
work at this speed because I had to pay attention to details while sculpting a figurine. But since I had sculpted the "Merry Wanderer" many,

many times, I didn't need to take time for special details. While I sculpted, I talked about production problems with certain figurines, or about myself, and answered questions from the audience. Collectors are always fascinated to see me convert a lump of clay into a figurine before their eyes, and when I was done with this figurine, some 25 minutes later, they applauded enthusiastically. I moved the modelling block back to the side of the room to provide a clear view of the screen for the movie.

For lunch, our guests enjoyed the famous Coburg bratwurst, a delicate sausage, and beer. At this time, I signed a lot of the Hummel figurines that the collectors had bought during their trip. Afterwards, they went on a sightseeing excursion to the Iron Curtain (which still existed then) and the old Veste (fortress) of Coburg; we did not see each other again until the Franconian party that evening.

The candlelight dinner in the giant hall of the Ehrenburg castle made a memorable finale to the trip, with music by a chamber ensemble, whose members were dressed in Roccoco costumes. After a souvenir photo session and a brief address given by me, we dined on a gourmet buffet.

Time passed far too quickly on this evening, and soon we had to say our farewells. Carrying colorful Chinese lanterns, we crossed the courtyard of the castle to the bus, which brought the guests back to the Goldene Traube, accompanied by our good wishes.

On my many promotional tours in the United States, I often met collectors who, even after many years, still raved about these Hummel Club trips. Some people took the tour several times, especially if there were different European cities on the itinerary. But for all of them, the stay in Coburg and the visit to the Goebel factory was the best part of their visit.

Night Launch

October 1985

The tension mounted. The crowd grew silent as the voice over the loud speaker began to count: "Nine, eight, seven, six, five, four, three, two, one, zero." The giant shuttle craft lifted off under full thrust, at first slowly, but then faster and faster into the dark sky, two fiery tails trailing it. I had witnessed the second night space-shuttle lift-off from the press section, a real vantage point. This impressive event was the fulfillment of a longtime dream.

During my involvement in astronomy in Berlin, I had become enthusiastic about space travel, which, at that time, seemed more like a utopian venture, and had joined the Society for Space Exploration. Rocketry pioneer Hermann Oberth was the honorary chairman, and Wernher von Braun was one of its members. Both men were instrumental in developing the V2 rocket at Peenemunde during World War II, which was considered the first step towards the realization of space travel. The United States and the USSR followed suit with their respective space programs. I followed the moon landings on television with the greatest interest, and dreamed of participating. I kept myself well informed of the latest developments by reading scientific books and magazines. But there is a big difference between learning about these great events secondhand and seeing them. I always had wanted to see and experience important things in person and I was successful most of the time. However, to fly around the earth in a space ship or to walk on the moon will remain dreams, with no chance of fulfillment. Watching a space shuttle launch close up will remain my ultimate personal experience in the fascinating field of space exploration.

It all started in Roedental, where once again I was hosting a group of M.I. Hummel Club members on the final evening of their trip. During the course of this happy "Franconian Evening." I met two ladies from Florida who were Hummel collectors. During our conversation, I discovered that one of them, Ann Conover, had a husband, Don, who worked for NASA in Cape Canaveral, Florida. My ears perked up. When Ann saw how interested I was, she immediately invited me to visit them in Cape Canaveral whenever a promotional tour might take me to Florida. The opportunity arose during the anniversary year. I scheduled a few "open" days for my visit to the Conovers and booked a motel room near Cape Canaveral. The motel was filled with people who had come to watch the launching of a space shuttle. I went to the Conovers' house on the shore to visit, and finally met Don. He invited me to stay with them, so I left the motel and moved in with this friendly family. After living in hotels for weeks on end, even though they were comfortable, I really appreciated staying in a private home! Ann proudly showed me her collection of M.I. Hummel figurines. While Don worked on a small airplane that he had built himself.

The next day I took a tour of the Cape Canaveral facilities, with Ann and her very energetic mother-in-law, Clara, as guides. The information offered to the interested public was really amazing. I was acquainted with many of the things on display, but I had never seen such a detailed and extensive exhibit; the movies, for example, were quite impressive.

On the following day, I flew around Cape Canaveral with Don in his small plane (which looked like an oversized model!) and I really enjoyed its mobility; the bird's-eye view of the launching facilities, with the ramps and huge hangars, was fascinating. In the afternoon we again drove to Cape Canaveral, but this time on a different road where we had to clear several checkpoints. Suddenly, I realized where had been a great misunderstanding on my part: I had incorrectly translated the Conovers' invitation. I couldn't understand why there would be such a to-do for just a "lunch." Only then, as we were walking to the press seats and I could see the shuttle being readied, did I see my error! I could hardly keep from laughing out loud.

A few weeks later, after my return to Coburg, I saw the terrible explosion and destruction of the Challenger shuttle on television. I was deeply affected by this tragedy. Later, I heard from Don that the commander of the shuttle had been a very good friend of his. It was almost incomprehensible to me that such a well-planned venture could end up as such a catastrophe. But it shows again that human efforts are always accompanied by certain unknown factors.

The Greatest Show

November 1985

There were so many people in the Hummel gift shop that I had a difficult time making my way through the crowd to the podium. I had done quite a number of promotions with large crowds on hand, but this one topped them all! I had never seen anything like this—it looked like half the population of Ohio had come to see me. It would be a very hard day for me, and I was still tired from the day before. I had signed the pre-sold figurines long into the night and had subsequently gone to bed very late. When Gunter Flegenheimer, the sales representative, first picked me up at the Cleveland airport, he warned me that this promotion would eclipse anything I had experienced before. He was right. David May, the shop owner, had planned everything perfectly. During the morning, three crews from the most important area television stations appeared and taped interviews with me. And it continued at this pace for the entire three days: signing, sculpting show, more hurried signing, and another sculpting demonstration. The store sales personnel constantly brought new trays filled with Hummel figurines to my table, and I signed and signed and signed my name underneath them all. A joker in the crowd said that I should apply for a space in *The Guinness Book of World Records*. Between demonstrations, I went back to the storage room, where shelf after shelf filled with Hummel figurines awaited my signature. It was really hard labor and I couldn't let on that I was practically exhausted. Some of the collectors had come from quite a distance, and so I did my best to be cordial to everyone; "keep smiling" was in vogue! It

145

certainly was a welcome change of pace when a television crew from Pittsburgh arrived in a helicopter and took me along for a short spin. From above, I could see that there was nothing but farmland surrounding David's store; that isolation made the establishment and success of one of the finest, largest Hummel gift shops in America even more remarkable.

For his next promotion, a few years later, David had a very nice surprise in store for me: For my welcoming, he had composed a song that was read and sung by his employees and the shop's visitors while he accompanied them on his organ. This "welcome" song, based on wellknown melodies, became such a hit, not only with me but with all the participants, that it had to be repeated several times a day. I taped it and played it back to my family and friends in Coburg, who enjoyed it as much as the visitors in Ohio.

Safari

November 1986

It seemed like a vision from a prehistoric era—but it was a reality. Hundreds of thousands of wild beasts surrounded us, as far as the eye could see. Toward the north, Mount Kilimanjaro, with its snow-covered peak, formed the background for this huge gathering of animals. They were grazing everywhere, filling the vast steppe clear up to the horizon. Among the dark-skinned animals could be seen zebras, somewhat lighter in color with their striping. Only a few spots overgrown with trees and brush were left ungrazed; there, the lions, sated and lazy, sunned themselves. Lions as well as hyenas would chase only the easy prey: young or sick animals. With an overabundance of food, the lions and hyenas were filled and left the other animals alone. Apparently, the animals knew exactly when the lions had no further appetite for them, and lost their shyness. We could spot from afar the places where the lions were devouring their meals; vultures circled overhead waiting for the leftovers.

We were a group of five participants in a safari driving in a Volkswagen bus with a sun roof through the Serengeti National Park in Tanzania. We were all deeply impressed with this awesome sight and tried to capture a small part of it with our cameras. We were in the right place at the right time, since wild-beast herds in huge numbers had just arrived from the north in their search for pastureland. This was the absolute climax of the safari, which again fulfilled a youthful dream of mine.

147

Two days before, we had been in the Ngorongoro crater and encountered practically all of the larger African animals during our excursions across the vast Caldera: elephants, rhinoceros, water buffalo, giraffe, lions, hyenas and *leopards*. We were able to get so close to them in the van that we could almost touch them. The numerous prides of lions, in particular, did not seem shy at all. We really enjoyed watching and photographing their family life. But we kept a safer distance from the rhinos and elephants because these animals, with their immense size, could be more dangerous to us if they felt threatened; they have been known to overturn or demolish a safari van. However, most of the animals ignored us; they had learned that the little white buses were no threat. It was tougher to approach the alert antelopes and the fleet-footed giselles, but we compensated for that by using binoculars and telephoto lenses. We were able to observe a dwarf gazelle the size of a dog for a very short time. Toward nightfall, we discovered a leopard mother with her three young ones consuming their meal. Finally, we returned to our hotel, which was situated at the rim of the crater. Cruising around in the crater at night is illegal; the harsh glare of headlights would disturb the animals.

During breakfast on the following morning, we could see the whole panorama of the giant crater through a picture window—a beautiful sight! The Ngorongoro crater, which is practically inaccessible, has remained a genuine sanctuary for the wild animals. (Due to the efforts of the famous German zoologist Bernhard Grzimek, the concept of national parks has gained a strong foothold in Africa. His final resting place is at the rim of the crater; his son, who died in a plane crash, is also buried there.)

On the way to the Serengeti, we also visited the Olduvai canyon where Leakey discovered one of the oldest specimens of man; the conclusion is obvious to me that the cradle of the human race was in Africa. I had a very special, but very annoying encounter in the Serengeti, at the Serena lodge. The area is populated with a large herd of pavians (apes). One evening, I rushed out to photograph an especially beautiful sunset and had forgotten to close the window in my room. I ran the entire length of the pathway through the garden, and had to turn a corner at the end of a building. I collided with the "chieftain" of the pavians. who also seemed to be in a hurry. He was not much smaller than I was, and we were both scared by this sudden collision. We stared at each other; then, the pavian leaped aside, with his mane flying, while I continued on my way, still a little groggy. On returning, I could hear a commotion and unintelligible screaming. When I reached my room, I saw the big mess: two young pavians, real mischief makers, had entered through the window and ransacked the room. My things were scattered all over the place. Outside, two hotel employees were chasing the apes and trying to wrestle my medicine bag away from them; the pavians were bitting into every box and tube, and then tossing them aside. It took quite some time before we had retrieved everything and tidied up. After this lesson, I always made sure that my door and windows were closed before I left the room.

The safari also took us to Lake Manyara, N.P., where we encountered many elephants in the primeval forest there. It is quite a sight to see a herd of pachyderms crash through the undergrowth, trampling whole trees to find the tenderest leaves. A typical primeval forest, with a stream traversing a clearing, stuck in my mind. When I paid a visit to my friend Hermann a short time later, I noticed he had a picture in his studio, painted from his imagination, that looked exactly like the stream in that forest. Today, the picture hangs in my studio, a reminder of my memorable safari to Africa.

After the safari had ended, I spent some time on a diving excursion at the turtle bay near Mombasa in Kenya, a place recommended to me by a American diver. Every day, with other diving enthusiasts, I made several dives to the coral reefs with their very opalescent underwater fauna. Only the Indo-Pacific oceans can match this colorful spectacle. My only regret was that Sieglinde could not accompany me on this journey.

In Pharaoh's Country

March 1987

We stood in a petrified forest, awed by the massive columns around us. They stood so close together that you could hardly see beyond them. Their bases, tapering towards the tops, gave these incredible pillars the appearance of tropical virgin forest trees. Who were these people who had built this Cyclopean temple of columns to honor their gods 3,600 years ago? It's difficult for us today to understand the philosophy of a long-lost culture. Even though we have learned a great deal about ancient Egypt by deciphering hieroglyphics, we can only be amazed by these structures, as we were at the Karnak temple near Luxor, the largest and most important of all Egyptian temples. These creations were built as a testimony to the gods.

Sieglinde and I again treated ourselves to the realization of a long-fostered, mutual dream: We were on an excursion through Egypt. We had always been attracted to this ancient culture, one of mankind's oldest. In our youth, long before we met, Sieglinde and I had both studied books about archaeological excavations in this country. Before Sieglinde was even born, I had admired reliefs and paintings at the Egyptian Museum in Berlin. I am sure that I was inspired by those museum visits and brought that inspiration into my own artistic work. I was particularly impressed with the masterly portraits created by ancient Egyptian sculptors, such as the famous bust of Nefertiti; very few objects of art have survived in so excellent a condition as this unique piece. In most instances, decay has destroyed the colors and, very often, the inlaid eyes, which originally looked so real. The ancient Egyptian belief that there was life after death, a life similar to that on earth, was the reason that gravesites were furnished more and more elaborately, to insure comfort in the hereafter. Man's greed and lust for gold, evident even in the age of the Pharaohs, have decimated the original splendor, with one exception: the tomb of King Tutankamen. The entrance to this tomb had been already been hidden in ancient times by sandstorms; the most precious treasure of Egypt was not discovered until this century. We were able to admire the thousands of priceless artifacts from this tomb during our visit to the Cairo Museum. If this young, politically unimportant king was buried in such a splendid tomb, imagine how much more lavishly appointed the tombs of the important Pharaohs had been!

I have always been interested in the art of ancient Egypt, but have especially admired the ancient sculptors, who created magnificent objects from the hardest granite with only the most primitive tools. I was also well read about the pyramids, one of the Seven Wonders of the Ancient World. Yet, when Sieglinde and I were standing in front of these monumental structures in Giza that were built more than 4,000 years ago, we were overwhelmed. I have always tried to see the most interesting sights in this world in person; my visit to the pyramids is proof that a description, no matter how well done, does not take the place of personal experience.

It is not only the long-lost culture that makes the land on the Nile so interesting; the people who live there today are friendly and peaceful. There is not another Islamic country that is less aggressive, and even though most Egyptians seem to lead very modest lifestyles, they appear to be content. I was very impressed by the Coptic monks in the desert west of the Nile delta, whose sect has lived a life of privation as hermits for 1,600 years; even so, they have been happy and fulfilled. One of my fondest memories of this trip was our tour guide through one of the oldest Christian cloisters. He had a friendly, imposing personality, and with his firm conviction in his own faith, was tolerant of others. For more than an hour, he told us the history of the convent, which had survived through the centuries despite constant threats by marauding Bedouin tribes. While I was listening to this monk, I felt as if there were an ancient prophet standing in front of me. The Copts are said to have almost completely retained the features of the ancient Egyptians.

On our second trip through this fascinating land I was accompanied by my daughter Suzanne. We traversed the Sinai Peninsula, with its red granite mountains and oases, so rich in history. On a moonlit night, we climbed to the top of the 8,000-foot Mount Sinai, where Moses was given the Ten Commandments by God, and we experienced a magnificent sunrise in this fantastic mountain world. I remained at the southern tip of the Sinai for another week, since I had planned to do some diving in the Red Sea, which has colorful underwater life. My daughter, quite impressed by all her experiences on this trip, flew home to Munich.

A Freelance Artist

June 1987

Now I was a freelance artist, and could pursue my creative interests at home whenever I pleased. Two years before, I had filed a claim for my pension and signed a contract with the Goebel company, which stated that I only had to work one-half of the time I had previously. There had been a few problems with my benefits, but these were quickly resolved. I was now my own boss; I determined the time I wanted to spend at the factory. This arrangement made it possible for me to use my time more efficiently. I set up a small studio at home, where I could work undisturbed. I even did without a telephone. My connection with Goebel remained through an exclusive contract, in which my duties and my rights were clearly spelled out.

Work in my studio was determined by a number of factors. Whenever I had scheduled appointments, such as a visit to the Siessen Convent or a pre-calculated date for the creation of a new figurine, I went to work immediately. In this way, I could spend a beautiful morning roaming the woods and, to compensate for that time, work late into the night. But since most of my commissions had been scheduled for some point in the future, I was able to work without being pressured by time constraints. Depending on my mood and state of mind, I could now model effectively and with concentration or I could wait to start until I felt right, especially when sculpting a new piece. A master should be in the proper frame of mind; only then can he create a good model. Many times, I crushed a clay model if it did not appear right to me and started over again when I was in a more creative mood. If I had adopted this practice while I was still an employee of Goebel, management might have frowned upon it. Simply put, it comes down to this: the time for which an employee is paid is different from that of a freelancer, who determines his own schedule for a project.

Since Germany's climate is such that we have only a short summer with not enough sunny, windy days, I would take off from work for a few days when the weather was good and spend the time with Sieglinde. We would either go sailing or swimming in our small lake or, if it was not warm enough for those activities, we would bicycle through the flat main valley. When I still worked full time, I could only occasionally spend time, mostly weekends, at our little "paradise," and very often we had rain or cold temperatures on Sunday. Now, I would work in my studio on rainy, cold weekends, and instead take time off during the week for my hobbies. Old age does bring us misery and an ebbing of our strength, but on the other hand, it has its pleasant sides, too.

Sieglinde and I both suffered from time to time from wanderlust, an urge to explore the world. Faraway places drew us like magnets, but we could rarely give in because of financial and time limitations. This had changed completely now. Our sons had their own interests and traveled with their friends on vacations. We were no longer tied down by school or factory vacation periods, and could travel whenever we wanted. Each trip was thoroughly planned; we studied books and attended travel seminars that pertained to the country we were going to visit. Since we were usually well informed about the culture, history and art of other countries, we traveled with a small group of like-minded people under the eye of a knowledgeable guide. We both took cameras along and competed with each other as to who could bring home the best photos of landscapes, landmarks and people. These trips also afforded me many inspirations for my artistic endeavors. We still found, in Germany and in Europe, areas with which we were not familiar. Nevertheless, whenever we returned to our home in Coburg, whether from a short or long journey, we found that home sweet home was still the best place to be.

In the "Living" Sea
October 1987

Slowly I slid down from the platform. After I had attached several additional pounds of lead to my belt, I could dive into the depths of an unusual underwater panorama. I was swimming amid several thousand fish in all sizes, shapes and colors, such as I had never found before in a coral reef: butterfly and trigger fish, arm-long angel fish, yard-long green parrot fish, giant groupers, schools of gold-lined rabbits. Beautiful arrangements of coral fish were swarming around me. Below, just above the bottom sponges, at a depth of almost 30 feet, swam a few seven-foot-long saw fish; above my head, sharks slithered through the water with hardly any movement, like torpedoes. About 20,000 fish populated this area, and that was no exaggeration—there were so many around me. But when I got closer to the reef, I saw that it was not living coral, but a plastic imitation.

With my friend Reece McCaine (at that time, one of Goebel's top salesman) and a diver from Disney World, I was swimming in the "living" sea, the largest aquarium in the world, located at Epcot Center in Florida. For Reece and me, it was a completely new experience in diving; not only were we observers of the beautiful underwater fauna, but we were being observed, ourselves. In the middle of this giant, ring-shaped aquarium were hundreds of tourists pressing their noses against the thick glass, watching: farther down, we could look into the restaurant, where diners could choose from a menu of freshly prepared fish (not from the aquarium, of course!). Why were we allowed to dive in the aquarium, limited strictly to divers employed by Disney World? As was so often the case, I had taken advantage of a sudden opportunity. In Reece's neighborhood, there lived a man named Kym Murphy, all underwater specialist of a unique sort. Having, been involved in the filming of *The Deep,* Kym had conceived of a "living" sea for Disney, the only attraction at Epcot Center that contained live animals. (All other Disney attractions are equipped with electronically guided dummies.) To accomplish this revolutionary idea, Kym had to use his entire bag of tricks to win over the Disney management. When I heard about this project, which required detailed planning and incredible technical requirements for its construction, I expressed my wish to dive in this aquarium once it was finished. Now my dream had come true when Kym invited us to this most unusual diving event that Reece and I will remember for the rest of our lives.

The Mayor
1988

I met Don Stephens for the first time in the sample room of the Goebel factory, when he showed me his newly acquired International M.I. Hummel figurines and asked me for authentication. In his quest for extremely rare Hummels, he had toured Germany, ending up in Roedental accompanied by his friends, Rue Dee Marker and Pat Arbenz. My eyes grew bigger and bigger as he unpacked more and more of these rare Hummel figurines and set them on the table in front of us. They were, without a doubt, all genuine and all in excellent condition. Curiosity got the better of me, and I asked Don where he found all these treasures. He just smiled and replied that he might tell me some other time. Evidently he didn't want to disclose this information prematurely, hoping to get more rarities from his source. I inspected each figurine closely and was able to assure Don that they were all authentic. This was easy to do, since I had only recently registered the International Hummel figurines in the Goebel factory archives, patching up small nicks and repairing some damage to them. Through competitive bidding, the prices of these rarities soared to five-digit figures. Don Stephens ranks among the greatest Hummel figurine collectors in the United States and he was very happy to expand his already large collection with the acquisition of this stately array of International Hummel pieces.

During my numerous trips to the United States and during his visits to Germany, I met Don again many times and we became friends. The basis of our friendship was his intense passion for collecting and his special interest in very rare figurines. Besides the M.I. Hummel figurines, Don also collects other Goebel products and the precious ANRI figurines. He consulted with me frequently; he would ask me for advice, especially when he was in the process of acquiring new and rare issues. So it was only natural that, over time, our relationship developed into a real friendship that included our families, too. We probably complemented each other because we had different professions, thus avoiding any competition, as may happen when friendships are based on the same area of interest.

Don's acquisitions developed, over the course of many years, into one of the most prominent M.I. Hummel figurine collections in the United States, as I mentioned before. But Don didn't want to keep the collection just for himself; he wanted to share it with others. So he donated the entire thing to the city of Rosemont, Illinois, which had a museum built in the reception hall of its convention center. As mayor of Rosemont, Don had recognized the favorable location of this small city adjacent to O'Hare airport and near many important highways, and had acted accordingly. Like America's Founding Fathers, Don converted a small village with just a few houses into a modern small metropolis. Rosemont today has an important convention center, a large sports arena, and towering hotels and skyscrapers. The crime rate is low, the economic base is sound, and so it is quite understandable that every American president visit this city while in office to honor Don Stephens as an exceptional mayor. The citizens of Rosemont, who have profited from these developments, hold their mayor in the highest esteem.

Every time that my travel schedule brings me to Chicago, I stay with Don. We take trips through the surrounding area, especially to a lake resort where Don owns a house. It is here that he keeps his motor boats. During one visit, we took a trip on the oldest boat in his collection, a 1920 model. After a while, we noticed that the mahogany hull was settling deeper and deeper in the water, so we returned to shore. Upon closer inspection, we found that the boat had sprung a leak and the water had almost flooded the engine. Since the leak would take some time to repair, we replaced the old boat with a sleek racing number and went out on the lake again, cruising on the crystal-clear water. Don also collects cars, especially Mercedes-Benz, and we often used one of his restored old-timers on our trips to Chicago, where we went to museums and other places of interest. The panoramic view from the top of the Sears Tower, the world's tallest building, is simply breathtaking, especially at sunset, when the last rays seem to cast a golden hue on Chicago's skyscrapers, and the huge lake, almost like an ocean, disappears into the night.

A Ship for Columbus's Anniversary—"Land in Sight"

1988

I was rejoicing inside, but tried to look composed on the outside. "That is exactly the motif for which I have searched for such a long time. Now I have found it," I told Bob Stiegler, who was looking over my shoulder as I leafed through an extensive collection of Hummel postcards. "It has to be a ship with many children on it, exactly like on this postcard, which I have never seen anywhere," I continued, pointing to the drawing on the postcard in front of me. I was very excited about it; this concept of a ship, filled with jubilant children, differed from all other drawings by Sister Maria Innocentia not only in its artistic flightiness but in its motif, too. And that was the main reason I liked this drawing instantly; I already anticipated the shape of the plastic model that I would create. The M.I. Hummel signature on the lower right-hand corner was proof that this was a drawing done by her. "Can you make me a copy of this?" I asked Bob. But he gave me the postcard and asked me to return it when I was finished with it. Once I returned to Germany, I would try to find another copy of it at the publishing house in Munich.

Bob Stiegler had invited me to stay at his house while I was in Kansas City so that I could verify the authenticity of two rare pieces that he had recently acquired. The entire Stiegler house is filled with M.I. Hummel figurines. Over the course of many years, Bob has amassed one of the largest Hummel collections that I have ever seen. He is especially proud of his many rarities, to which he is always adding new ones. I was able to confirm that his recent (and very costly) acquisitions, the "Papa" and "Mama" figurines, were authentic, much to his great satisfaction.

For a while, we discussed certain questions that collectors of Bob's magnitude have before turning to his collection of Hummel post-cards, which is supposedly complete. (Apparently, this is the case because I saw many cards that have been out of circulation for quite some time before I spotted the ship card.) As I learned later, during a visit to the Siessen Convent, Maria Innocentia had given this draw-ing to an acquaintance as a birthday present, and the postcard had been printed in Munich for only a very short time. I was able to ob-tain a copy from the publishing house's archives, and returned the original postcard to Bob.

As soon as I possibly could, I began work on the model, making rapid progress, since I had already visualized the finished figurine. I started with the ship's hull before modeling the sails and seating the children inside. I could not put all the children into the figurine; not only would that have led to a lot of production problems, but it would have raised the cost of the figurine tremendously. So, I decided to place only four children in the ship as its crew. Being an active sailor myself, I had to put a helmsman at the rudder, which would prob-ably be located behind the big sail, as Sister Hummel's sketch indi-cated. The other three children symbolize Columbus's great discov-ery in the nicest way possible: While the child with the trumpet greets the New World with a blast from his instrument, the second child waves the flag, and the third strews flowers into the sea from a horn of plenty, a symbol of the riches and resources of this new land. It was almost as if Sister Maria Innocentia had had a premonition of the future use of this picture—she had included all of these activities in her drawing. I am sure she would have been delighted with the finished figurine.

The model was well received at the convent, but Sister Witgard insisted on a fifth child in the boat. So I created the smallest child, who looks down to the fish, oblivious to the importance of America's discovery. In a way, this symbolizes the ever-present ignoramuses who have always been and always will be around, who do not recognize the significance of an era.

From the beginning of this project, my opinion was that the ship figurine should be issued in 1992 as a limited and numbered issue to commemorate the 500th anniversary of Christopher Columbus' discovery of America in 1492. This would be the only way to do justice to a piece that is so unique and so different from all the others. For the past ten years, I have made a special effort to create models that are clearly different in motif from the rest of the figurines, particularly, I think, "Chapel Time" and "Let's Tell the World." However, none of these will ever come close to "Land in Sight."

Gone with the Wind
May 1988

The red rock formation came closer and closer, or rather we floated towards it until we could almost touch it. Then my companion yanked on a cord, and with a whooshing noise, a giant flame shot up above our heads. We rose up a few feet and floated over the rock formation; we were then able to look down on the meadows far below us, glistening in the dew. It was a beautiful feeling of freedom, free from the earth's gravity as we sailed along in the cool morning air, with only our shadow trailing us below over fields and meadows. We, the pilot and I, floated—only motor-powered aircraft fly—in a hot-air balloon over the red cliffs of Sedona in northern Arizona.

Once again, a dream became reality: to float noiselessly in the gondola of a balloon (even though the reheating of the air made quite a racket). But nothing diminished our enthusiasm when we were sailing the morning breeze over a beautiful landscape. Red rocks and cliffs in fantastic shapes were interspersed with overgrown hills, like a giant backdrop of a stage. I thought I could see the Grand Canyon to the north, into which I had already descended twice and which again seemed to attract me as if by magic.

After a promotion in Phoenix, I had taken a few days off to visit some extraordinary attractions that I had always passed by on my way to the Grand Canyon. But when I wanted to rent a car at the Phoenix airport, I couldn't find my credit card. I must have lost it or misplaced it, because despite a thorough search of all pockets and wallet, it was not to be found. It's almost impossible to rent a car without a credit

card and, and I was denied a car at the Avis counter as well as at Hertz.
I was quite discouraged and about to give up on my trip north, when
I decided to try one last time at Dollar Rental. An attractive young
lady looked at me with obvious interest as I explained my dilemma.
Then a smile of recognition came over her pretty face and she spoke
my name. A collector of Hummel figurines, she had seen my face in
photographs and in several books. I would get a car from her without a credit card, but as a personal favor, she asked for my picture,
which I signed for her. Once in the designated parking lot, though,
I didn't find the compact car I had requested, but a very nice mid-size
car. I returned to the nice woman to explain the mistake. But she
said, "Well, do you think I would give you just a compact?" She acted
as if she were almost offended by the thought, so I started my trip
north in a comfortable car.

After a roundabout trip to places such as the Petrified Forest,
the Painted Desert and the meteor and sunset crater, I arrived in
Sedona and made an appointment with the balloon pilot for the next
morning. At a very early hour, we made our preparations from an
empty parking lot. The balloon's hull had been spread out in the lot,
and was pumped up by a ventilator; then the air inside the balloon
was heated by a gas burner, until the balloon began to rise. Then,
after the customary champagne had been loaded aboard, it was time
to climb into the gondola, which was steadied by two assistants. The
order came to release the lines, and we rose swiftly into the fresh
morning air. A light breeze carried us to the famous rocks of Sedona.
The two assistants, who kept contact with us by radio, followed us in
a truck, making sure that they didn't lose us. After almost an hour of
"float" time, we landed next to a small road, but had to work our way
out of a tree top before we had solid ground beneath our feet again.
This thrilling episode ended without much of a hitch; after the bouncy
trip back in the truck, with the balloon in tow, I received a certificate
for my first balloon ride.

Since I still had most of the day ahead of me, I got into the car
without further ado and headed for the Grand Canyon. By the time
I arrived there, it was too late to go down to the Colorado River, so
instead, I took the Kaibab trail downwards, one with which I was
unfamiliar. Time and again I have been fascinated by the colorful
display of lights and shadows in the Canyon, and this trip was no

exception. I was able to take many photographs of this beautiful scenery. On the way up, the sun was sinking deeper in the sky; the violet-blue shadows cloaked the gorges in a mysterious darkness, and the rock castles, formed by erosion, glowed a deep copperred. I could absorb the magic atmosphere and it was hard to tear myself away from this fantastic panorama. But finally, I started back to Sedona.

An Army of Clay

February 1989

There they stood in front of us—the clay soldiers of the army of
Emperor Qin Shi Huang—looking at an imaginary enemy. They almost
looked alive, these giant warriors who had guarded their departed chief
beneath the surface of the earth for more than 2,000 years. They stood
in rank and file, in full armor with every detail and the insignia of rank.
No face was alike; each head had its own characteristics. More than
1,000 figures had been excavated, and remained in the places where
they had been found. There were supposed to be more than 6,000 of
them, most still buried. A huge hall had been built over the excavation site to protect the clay soldiers from the weather. A farmer had
discovered the first head and other parts in 1974 while plowing a field
near Xian in central China; when the experts began to excavate, this
sensational archaeological miracle came to light.

As a colleague of the 2,000-year-old artists who made these soldiers,
I was fascinated by the figures, and wanted to learn every detail about
the creation of these statues, whose life-like appearance had been
enhanced by painting in natural colors. The workshops of these ancient
artists, containing molds and forms, had been discovered, enabling the
archaeologists to deduce precisely how these warriors and their horses
had been created. In order to avoid a stereotypical look, the artists had
modeled ten different types of heads; they then made molds from the
models after the ears had been removed. The resulting prototype heads
were then individually decorated. Through the addition of beards and
very detailed hairstyles, the artists created so many different types of
heads that you had to look long and hard to find some that looked

alike. The ravages of time had not left much of the colors in which these soldiers were painted. But if you can imagine that, through painting, the individualization had been even greater and more impressive, what a lifelike atmosphere must have emanated from these soldiers when they were finished and displayed! This discovery will be profoundly important for history and research, since the figures in their different uniforms, hairstyles and weapons surely represent various tribes, sculptured as they were from living models. The tomb of the emperor, which is more than a mile from the site of the figures, has not yet been touched by archaeologists, even though spectacular finds are expected. This task will be left to the next generation.

During our trip to China, which happened only a short time before the bloody events in Tianamen Square in Beijing, we took in many other sights of this vast country. To us, the Imperial Palace, with its 999 rooms, was very impressive. Since heaven, for the Chinese, has 1,000 rooms, the palace is restricted to 999 of them. The Great Wall of China, the largest structure on earth, has been completely restored to a length of several miles north of Beijing. We walked on the road atop the Wall, which is interlaced with guard towers and which runs uphill and downhill, until we could go no further because of cave-ins and erosion. Visitors from all parts of China and tourists from around the world made a colorful display on the road. It is really amazing how this immense wall snakes through steep mountains; we could understand why this is the only man-made structure visible by the naked eye from the moon. Near Beijing, a majestic boulevard lined with large statues of animals and guardians led to the tombs of the Ming emperors. I was impressed with the size of the figures as well as the many detailed paintings in the corridor of the summer palace.

Many Chinese paintings show landscapes with steep mountains, which are often taken for exaggerated fantasy on the part of the artists. However, we observed this fantastic landscape in the southern part of the country during an excursion on the Li River that lasted several hours. Steep, overgrown mesas that surrounded us seemed to move together and then apart, constantly revealing new vistas, like props on a giant stage. Fishing villages and caves draped with lianas moved by us, while fishermen on bamboo rafts glided silently past, with cormorants, trained to catch fish, perched on the rafts. Our trip through China gave us insights into one of man's oldest cultures and impressed us with the hospitality of its people.

Mount Palomar

October 1989

A youthful dream was becoming a reality. I was standing in front of the large, 15-foot telescope that pointed majestically skyward. I wasn't behind the glass enclosure that kept visitors quite a distance away from the precious instrument, but right next to it. The telescope is impressive, not only because of its gigantic dimensions but also because of its unique construction. Our host, Professor Christian Tinney from the Mount Palomar Observatory, saw my admiring eyes staring up and said, "If you want to climb up there, I will open the large mirror for you." He did not have to repeat his offer; I was already on my way up. Climbing to the high observation platform was child's play for an experienced mountain climber such as myself. From that height, looking down on the huge mirror as it opened, I could really comprehend the true size of this enormous instrument. Nearby was the giant cupola that guarded the telescope from the elements when it was not in use. It was an awe-inspiring moment. I thought back to my youth in Berlin as a member of the astronomical society there, when I had the opportunity to inspect construction drawings for the erection of this telescope. Later, I read articles about the casting and the polishing of the main mirror. With great interest, we all followed through the various astronomical publications the construction of the telescope, with its new, horseshoe-like mounting. However, my wish to see the finished telescope in operation could not be answered because of the war. Now, in the later years of my life, my old dream had become reality. It took a long, long time before I could tear myself away from this spectacular sight and make my descent.

As so often has happened in my life, circumstances and luck came together. Before starting my promotional tour in the United States, I had asked my friend Mario to arrange a trip to Mount Palomar on my day off, after the promotion at his Collector's World in Montrose. He agreed, and the day after the successful promotion, we drove south through the wonderful mountains. A beautiful, sunny morning helped us forget the stress of the past few days. En route we visited the old mission of Pala, built when California was conquered by the Spaniards. We ambled through the old, primitive rooms of the convent and the church, impressive reminders of the days when the first Europeans settled there. The flower beds in the cloister were in full bloom and I visualized the old Spanish monks making their rounds in measured steps while saying their prayers. But we had to press on since, as Mario pointed out, our visit to Mount Palomar had been arranged for a certain time. When we saw a sign that read "Antiques," though, we just had to stop. Both Mario and I got great pleasure from snooping around in antique shops. You never knew if you might run across something interesting and valuable. While Mario was searching far old signs, steins and jugs, I devoted my time to inspecting local rarities and Indian jewelry.

After a long journey, the road gradually became steeper, winding itself with many curves and turns to the top of Mount Palomar. Once at the summit, we first enjoyed the beautiful panoramic view of the surrounding mountains. But I could wait no longer, and soon we were on our way to the dome that housed the telescope, the tallest building there. At a side entrance, we were greeted by Professor Tinney, whom Mario had contacted about our impending visit. We started on our tour, guided by an expert who showed us all the rooms in the observatory and explained their various functions. The electronic age had arrived, and new methods of measuring were being used. Here at Mount Palomar new and far-reaching information about the structure as well as the creation of the universe had been uncovered with the gigantic telescope. After the tour, I made my memorable ascent to the large instrument while my two companions downstairs wondered if I would ever come back. Of course, I would have loved to have explored a planet with this majestic "eye," but that was out of the question; we would have had to remain overnight and

I had to catch a plane early the next morning. Since the telescope is used primarily for the photographic exploration of the stars, it's possible that a visual observation would have been quite disappointing.

As a small token of our appreciation, we presented Professor Tinney with the Hummel figurine "The Stargazer," to which I had added a personal inscription and my signature. He was very happy with this gift and promised to give it a prominent place in his studio at the observatory. The memorable day came to an end. We descended the road headed toward Los Angeles. Once again, we couldn't resist stopping at several antique shops to snoop around.

The Disney Project
June 1990

There they were, all lined up in a spectacular exhibit, the first Disney figurines from the 1950s, created here in Roedental through personal contact between Franz Goebel and Walt Disney. Here at the Disney archives in Los Angeles, the figurines were treated with a special reverence; they were the first three-dimensional ceramic characters based on those from the Disney animated movies.

I had not participated in the creation of these first Disney pieces because I had only been working for Goebel a very short time. But I remember that I had fashioned the mother molds for some of these models. The Goebel figurines were not the only things in the Disney archives, of course, but they certainly were a distinguished group as compared to all the other figurines from other parts of the world that had been added over time. There were some made of wood, glass and metal, but most of them were made of ceramic, many in the Orient; almost all were colorfully painted. Among the more expensive, elaborate samples were also some that had been cheaply molded in one piece. I looked at all these figurines very carefully, while at the same time I listened to the eloquent explanations from the woman in charge of the archives. But what was the real reason I was here at the Disney archives in far-away Los Angeles?

During a very secret meeting with Goebel's top management in the spring of 1990, I was offered the chance to participate in the development of the Disney project. Disney and Goebel had agreed to do it, with the ultimate goal being the creation of a collection of figurines of all the Disney characters, pieces for collectors that would be of high quality. As Art Director, my job was primarily the coordination of our team and the Disney development team. I do not like short trips of a few days' duration over vast distances, but this time I had to make an exception and endure the long flight to Los Angeles. My first contacts with Disney management and the people with whom I would later work were very important.

When I had been given this opportunity a few weeks earlier, I finally agreed to it, after spending some time considering all its aspects. My main concern was that the stress that comes with such a major undertaking might be too much for a person of my age. On the other hand, of course, I was attracted to the project's challenges, so I decided to do it. From the very beginning, I realized that our greatest problem would be the cost of manufacturing these figurines, and therefore a relatively high retail price. Later on, my suspicions were confirmed and eventually the production was done abroad.

During my year-long involvement in the Disney project, I met many interesting people, and received an inside view of this gigantic enterprise with the Disney name, perhaps the only one of its kind in the world. Time and again I was deeply impressed by this perfect organization, where nothing was left to chance; every detail, no matter how minute, was thoroughly thought through and discussed.

I tried to achieve the best results during my Disney tenure in transforming these well-known animated characters into three-dimensional figurines, with the close cooperation of the Goebel development team and with the guidance of the Disney experts. Occasionally, when there were very difficult models, I lent a hand to the creation of these figurines. All my colleagues from the Goebel team worked on the project with great enthusiasm, and were able to overcome all difficulties and problems. It wasn't easy: the objective here was not only the transformation of drawings, as was the case with M.I. Hummel figurines; we had to transpose comic characters from movies into three dimensions while preserving and expressing their funny movements that had made these characters so famous around the world. We had great support from the Disney team, but we also often encountered differences of opinion—something that had been approved one day could be thrown out the next.

The stress that I had so dreaded in the beginning became at times very prevailing, and so I was quite happy when all models had been completed satisfactorily and my share in this project came to an end.

The Wallstreet Engagement
1992 and 1993

As I stood in front of this long wall, I was contemplating what in the world I could do with these modern windows, which stretched over the entire 180 feet of this corridor. This seemingly endless row of windows above me, right under the ceiling, presented a problem which I had cast aside long enough, and now I had to cope with it and solve it. How could I incorporate these windows into a colorful project that matched the opposing, but windowless, wall? For this wall I had designed a long row of romantic houses and enlivened them with people, dogs and cats.

This long row of flat windows reminded me of the old agricultural estates in my native Franconia where the barn and stable buildings often had similar windows. Stable windows—that was the correct idea for this project! If I encased them with massive bricks, I could change the appearance of this modern windows to such an extent that they would lose their modern functions, and seem to be several hundred years older.

Back in my hotel room, I went to work immediately. After a few rough sketches I visualized how I could work out the painting on this wall: Windows, doors and gates, all encased by medieval-looking bricks, enlivened by a wall fountain, booths and benches, occupied by people, would fit in nicely with the romantic houses on the opposite wall.

Thus I created with my crayon the massive stables and barns on a large German farm which covered the entire wall space. One barn-door was shown open and inside the barn one could catch a glimpse of a fully loaded hay-wagon. When I showed these sketches later on to Katherine, the interior architect, she was very enthusiastic about my work and offered ideas of her own to further enrich the scenery. In the hay-wagon was to sit a pair of lovers, and the wall of the estate was not to run the entire length of the wall. It would expose a beautiful landscape beyond the boundaries of the farm. I readily accepted her ideas and made the corresponding designs. At the end of the wall a flock of sheep was wandering into the Franconian landscape towards the ruin of an old castle.

How did it come about that I, a sculptor, was engrossed in the creation of a mural? The story begins with one of my visits to Rosemont, near Chicago. My friend, mayor Donald Stephens, had remarried. Katherine, a very talented interior architect, had been commissioned with the development of the O'Hare Expo Center. In this capacity, Don had met, and fallen in love with, her. Katherine, with her elegant taste and natural instinct for shapes and colors, had given the Convention Center an exquisite appearance. Many areas of the Expo Center were connected by long walk-ways or corridors: Katherine found their white-washed walls simply boring. So one day Don asked me if I could make some sketches for a colorful and more appealing appearance of these white walls. As an American of German origin, Don was thinking of motifs such as villages and landscapes in Germany. Since I had not endeavored to make any murals and paintings for a long time, I wanted some time to mull this over.

But back in Coberg I found my curiosity aroused by this project and started to develop my first sketches and drawings. The more I became engrossed in this project the more I seemed to catch fire and enjoyed it. I sent my designs to Katherine, made changes, created new ones, and finally I hit on the idea to create a street with old German buildings.

On my next visit to Rosemont, in the spring of 1993, I sketched several houses on the wall in their original size with charcoal and colored crayons, in order to test their effect. After I received a very positive reaction from both Don and Katherine, I began studying old houses upon my return to Germany. I did many preliminary sketches and drew a detailed color design on an 18-foot roll of paper, in a scale of 1:10. It showed a street in a small German town with a hotel, Rathaus (City Hall), Bakery, Wine-room, and many old romantic houses in their medieval frame-work. I enlivened the scenery with people, among them Don, Katherine and Don's grandchildren. Later I added a manager from the Expo Center too.

I then transferred the individual houses on single sheets of paper and send them to Don and Katherine, who gave a whole-hearted endorsement to this project, which I called "Wallstreet."

In the fall of 1993, just prior to my promotional tour of the U.S., the project became a reality. A team of five artists, all with long-time experience in murals, set out to transfer my design onto the walls. It was a job with a lot of problems, and quite often I had to make changes which were caused by the enlargement to ten times the size of my design. The artists did a splendid job, and often passers-by stopped and commented very favorably about the project.

After three weeks, everything had progressed so rapidly that I was able to take a short vacation before beginning on my tour. I met my nephew Chris from San Francisco in the Caribbean and we spent a fantastic vacation scuba diving at an atoll on the barrier reef in Belize.

At the end of my "tour" I made a detour to Chicago, and admired the almost completed "Wallstreet." It gave me tremendous joy to create something completely different. In an active life, learning just never stops.

QVC Show
1993

A letter from Goebel Marketing Corporation had arrived. In it, Joan Ostroff informed me that I was to participate in a live show of the home Shopping Channel QVC during my promotional tour of the USA in the fall.

My first reaction was to refuse participation in such a show. To sell collectibles and quality products, as the M.I. Hummel figurines had been for decades, via the television screen, seemed incomprehensible to me. How could it be possible to replace the personal touch and conversation with the individual customer and collector with a television screen? But then my curiosity took over, and I decided to form my own opinion and judgement on this type of selling. So, I agreed, even though I was very skeptical, to participate in the QVC show.

To my great surprise, a complete film team from QVC arrived in Germany a few weeks later, in order to shoot some video tapes. At the factory in Roedental, at the convent in Siessen and in Massing (the birthplace of Sister M.I. Hummel) film shots were taken, filled with Hummel figurines. All the manufacturing processes, such as sculpting, moldmaking, casting and mounting, firing and painting were thoroughly and professionally filmed. Really, I had not expected such a detailed study from a merchandising channel but now I looked forward to my participation in the QVC show with great anticipation.

At the end of October, after my promotional tour through the USA, I spent two free days in Philadelphia and stayed at the Bond

House, a very stylish bed and Breakfast Inn from the 18th century. Right around the corner was the famous "Bookbinders" seafood restaurant, where I really enjoyed a delicious Maine lobster.

On Friday I was driven to our hotel in Westchester, where Joan Ostroff, Gwen Toma and I huddled together for a very detailed discussion about the upcoming television show. Three shows had been scheduled: one each of 20 minutes in length at midnight (9 p.m. pacific time), and again the following morning, and also a three-hour show on Saturday afternoon. I was to sculpt the Hummel figurine #331 "Crossroads." For this purpose, I had black clay shipped to the USA.

Quite a party gathered for dinner on this Friday. Besides us three, there was Ken LeFevre, the QVC hosts Bob Bowersox and Dan Wheeler, as well as the purchasing agents, Beth Coleman and Nancy Panccio. This was the first opportunity for me to meet with the most important QVC personnel, especially with Bob Bowersox, and to establish personal contact in a leisurely atmosphere and not during the hectic hustle and bustle of an ongoing show. Right from the the beginning, we got along very well, and I looked ahead to my appearance on the show in a cool and composed manner.

Around 10 p.m. we drove over to the QCV studios where we already were expected. I was very impressed by the equipment and organization in the studio; it compared favorably with the many television studios that I had seen in the past 18 years. A revolving stage allowed a rapid change of scenery, the cameras and lighting were steered from a central console, and batteries of telephones were ready to take orders. In a lounge we were able to see the ongoing broadcasts, and in a dressing-room we were "beautified" by a make-up artist.

All the shows, were conducted with a profound knowledge of the product and very good information, and even the entertainment element was not shortchanged. Questions which were called or faxed in by customers to us were answered during the broadcast. With all these positive aspects, my original skepticism turned into real enthusiasm and the following years I participated in other very successful QVC shows.

The greatest satisfaction for me is, however, when I meet Hummel collectors during my regular promotions who tell me that they started collecting through the QVC shows, and that they are now looking for more M.I. Hummel figurines at regular dealers. Very often I am greeted with the words "I have seen you on QVC."

The Future

Even at the age of 73, I don't think you should dwell on the past. If you are lucky enough to have had long-living ancestors, the possibility of many more fulfilling years is simply great. In order to enjoy this last chapter of life in a relatively independent way, you have to help yourself. The basic, fundamental requirements for a carefree old age are healthy nutrition, exercise, many hobbies and an open mind, even a certain curiosity, about changes in our world. Most important, however, is a positive attitude towards life, and the ability to enjoy every moment. Don't let the unavoidable little aches and pains of old age bother you too much. The much-quoted "Wisdom of Age," which, of course, differs from one person to the next, can be attained in this way. And you should still have dreams, those that are attainable and those that will never be fulfilled. I am very grateful that fate has spared me the abrupt, often very painful transition into retirement. As long as I possibly can, I will continue my artistic endeavors and try to bring happiness to my fellow man with them. I sincerely hope that I will be able to sculpt new models in the years ahead, and I am sure that most of them will be M.I. Hummel figurines. I will strive to find unusual motifs drawn by Maria Innocentia and new methods to achieve this goal.

Besides my work as an artist, I have always been close to nature, and interested, too, in science and technology. Because of this, I have come to realize how much our lifestyle has changed in a highly technological world, changed in a way that is no longer justifiable to future generations. The aura of "happy childhood," so vividly expressed by the M.I. Hummel figurines, with their flowers and animals and tranquil nature, will soon cease to exist if we continue to ruin the fundamental structure of our world. For reasons of convenience, greed, egotism and ignorance, we irresponsibly allow the atmosphere, water and the earth to become poisoned and destroyed. We must change our habits radically, before it is too late, unless we are prepared to leave to our children a world in which they can only exist in a vegetative state caused by sickness. In recognition of this problem, I have joined the Green Peace movement, and support it wholeheartedly. This organization, through spectacular actions and often shocking disclosures, has contributed greatly to people's environmental awareness and has laid the foundation for a new way of thinking about the environment. We all must learn that consumption is not everything, and that we must carefully conserve those things that cannot be replaced. We can't afford to continue poisoning the earth. Those terrible legacies, the nuclear bombs, of the insane armament programs established during the Cold War, which was ended by Russian president Gorbachev, must be destroyed in such a way that the environment will not be harmed. Only then can we pass on to our heirs a world in which they can live, and preserve for them the wholesome atmosphere of which the M.I. Hummel children are symbols.